the Power of Metaphor

Story Telling & Guided Journeys for
Teachers, Trainers & Therapists

MICHAEL BERMAN AND DAVID BROWN

Crown House Publishing Limited
www.crownhouse.co.uk

First published in the UK by

Crown House Publishing Limited
Crown Buildings
Bancyfelin
Carmarthen
SA33 5ND
UK
www.crownhouse.co.uk

First published 2000; reprinted 2001

British Library of Cataloguing-in-Publication Data
A catalogue entry for this book is available
from the British Library.

ISBN 1899836438

Printed and bound in Wales by
Gomer Press
Llandysul

I would like to thank my mother, Ketevan, and friends,
as well as my Helpers in non-ordinary reality, for all
their support and for helping me to make this book possible.
I would also like to thank everyone at
Crown House Publishing for believing in the project.
M.B.

With gratitude to all the people,
places and stories that have inspired me.
Thank you.
D.B.

Table of Contents

Acknowledgments

The authors thank the following for permission to reproduce copyright material:

Kogan Page Ltd for permission to use an adapted version of *Giant Steps* taken from *Tales for Trainers* by Margaret Parkin.

Network Educational Press for permission to use an extract from *Accelerated Learning in the Classroom* by Alistair Smith.

Alawn Tickhill for the *Tree Poems* taken from a magazine called *Medicine Ways* issue 4.

Jessica Kingsley Publishers Ltd for *The Healing Waters* taken from *Storytelling in Education and Therapy.*

HarperCollins Publishers, Inc for *The Great Smoking Mirror* from *Sacred Path Cards* by Jamie Sams.

Roger Jack for *The Pebble People* taken from the collection *Earth Power Coming* published by the Navajo Community College Press.

Introduction

In this book you will find a collection of stories, ancient and modern, and journeys of the imagination that can lead you through the story that your life was meant to be.

Stories have always been a powerful tool for communicating information from one generation to the next and for educating the young. If they were not highly successful for this purpose, the art of story telling would not have survived.

Whenever people meet, stories are told and they have been told since time immemorial. Story telling is an oral tradition and because of the issues which have been worked through by the telling of the stories, story telling has contributed to the creation of the great epics of the world. The storytellers themselves have been described as the bridge to other times, and ancient teachings and the telling of the stories helps to keep these teachings alive. The children of future generations learn from the storytellers and apply lessons of the stories to their own lives.

The earliest stories were probably chants or songs of praise for the natural world in pagan times. Later, dance and music accompanied stories. The storyteller would become the entertainer for the community and the historian, musician and poet too. The oral tales that were passed on from one generation to the next by word of mouth included epics, myths, parables, fables, fairy tales and folk tales.

The art of story telling was particularly popular from around AD 400 to 1500. Storytellers would travel around visiting markets, villages, towns and royal courts. They gathered news, swapped stories and learned regional tales in the process. When popular tales began to be printed cheaply in pamphlets known as chapbooks and sold by pedlars, their popularity started to wane. With the advent of the mass media, the storyteller has unfortunately become more or less extinct.

Story telling is also an effective vehicle to deliver messages to the subconscious where the 'aha's of metaphor take place. It is our ability to make metaphorical connections that allow us to learn anything at all. When something new is like something we've done before, we take what we know from the first situation and transfer our knowledge to the new situation. Metaphor instils the learning of content or process on a very subtle, often subconscious level. When the subconscious is activated or accessed, the material enters the mind with no resistance. As a result, metaphors can effect dramatic change in an individual.

Each time you ask someone to stretch their awareness of time and space you are inducing a light state of trance and each story that starts with "Once upon a time" provides an example of this.

A story can be called a metaphor if the listeners can relate to it and draw a parallel between the action in it and their own lives. It has been suggested that if a picture is worth a thousand words, then perhaps we can regard a metaphor as being worth 1000 pictures.

According to psychologists, our memories seem to work best when we can see things as part of a recognised pattern, when our imaginations are aroused, when we can make natural associations between one idea and another, and when the information appeals strongly to our senses. An imaginative story, rich in vocabulary, that appeals to the senses, which works as a metaphor, and is cumulative in nature, clearly fulfils all these criteria. Cumulative tales have definite stages and in each stage characters and activities are added on. The result is a rhythm and a repetition which is hypnotic in quality. This helps to induce alpha brainwaves and the optimal state for learning and remembering. The process can also bring about a form of regression to childhood days and recreate in us that emotional state of curiosity, which as adults we tend to lose.

It is emotions, not logic, that drive our attention, meaning-making and memory. This suggests the importance of eliciting curiosity, suspense, humour, excitement, joy and laughter. Story telling can provide an ideal means of achieving this.

If you're shy at the thought of reading stories aloud, try the following: record the story and play it back for yourself; climb a hill out in the forest and read it to a tree or some kindly squirrels; or tell it to yourself in the shower or in your car. If you can tell a story rather than read it, this leaves your hands free to gesture, allows you to make eye contact with your audience and to calibrate for their responses.

An example of how story as metaphor can be used in an educational setting is presented below. It was designed for students of English as a Foreign Language about to embark on a course in the UK, to promote positive expectations.

The Learning Place

This is the story of Alessandra, a young woman who leaves her parents' home to make her own way in the world. She's looking for something more than the familiar everyday routine of her family, the challenge of the new and unfamiliar. So she travels to the Learning Place, a special place visited by seekers of all kinds, in the land known as Dan Glen. She arrives in autumn, just as the leaves are beginning to change to colours of deep red, orange and yellow, and the trees themselves are turning within for the winter.

Alessandra's feeling a bit nervous because she's never been to Dan Glen before and doesn't understand the language spoken there. So when she arrives and hears the people speaking so quickly, she gets frightened and thinks perhaps she's made a big mistake. Many learners are based in the Centre besides herself and she notices they don't appear to be afraid. In fact, they seem to be enjoying life to the full and this helps to reassure her.

Alessandra walks around the Centre feeling rather lost until she meets one of the welcome guides who helps new arrivals to feel at home. The guide's name is Karelov. Karelov is a kind, gentle man who soon makes her feel comfortable listening to his native language. She's surprised at how relaxed and confident she feels with her guide. Her understanding of the new language grows quickly, and before long she's beginning to use the language too. Karelov recognises that Alessandra has all the abilities she needs to do very well.

With Karelov's support and encouragement, Alessandra begins to open her mind and heart to all the new opportunities around her. Karelov spends many hours with Alessandra and the other new arrivals. He tells them lots of stories, he plays lots of games and listens with patience and interest. They all learn quickly without even realising it's happening and Alessandra's confidence quickly grows. She makes friends with the other new arrivals in her group and she recognises that their situations are similar to her own.

One of these friends, Eduardo, invites her to the annual festival of dance in Dan Glen. Karelov has taught them the traditional dances and they demonstrate their skills at the festival with ease and delight. Even the natives are impressed and congratulate them on the naturalness and ease of their performance.

During one of the breaks, a traditional dance instructor called Killjoy asks them how many hours and days they must have struggled to reach such a high standard. He can't believe it when they tell him that it was no struggle at all and that they enjoyed every minute of it. He thinks they must be lying. Alessandra and Eduardo become a little confused and wonder if they did something wrong. They can't understand all this analysis of their learning which just happened so naturally.

At this moment Karelov and his partner Bella, who are also attending the dance, invite the young couple to join them in a dance for four. They tell Karelov about their conversation with the old dance instructor and Karelov smiles. He explains that unfortunately there are still teachers like Killjoy in the Centre with old-fashioned beliefs about how learning takes place. Killjoy, it seems, has forgotten that learning can be an enjoyable experience and that when people feel relaxed they can produce their best work. Alessandra and Eduardo realise from their own recent experiences that what Karelov is saying is true and a smile of recognition appears on the young couple's faces as they join Karelov and his partner for the dance.

The next day Karelov announces to Alessandra and the rest of the group that their initiation is now complete. They have all mastered naturally and with ease a basic understanding of the language and they are ready to move on. Their understanding of themselves and others has grown and so has their confidence. The friendships will last, the pleasant memories will remain, and the ending is just a beginning. As Karelov concludes his remarks, he invites everyone to hold hands and to join him in a circle, a circle of strength and unity.

Alessandra has since become a fine teacher herself and Eduardo is now working as an interpreter. And we leave them to continue their journey through life, following easily and naturally the best guide of all – the Karelov who resides within them.

Each of the stories presented in this collection is followed by a script for guided visualisation. These can be used with individual clients and/or when working with groups. The rest of this introduction deals with the background to, and the benefits to be derived from, the use of this technique.

Neuro-Linguistic Programming (NLP) has made us aware of the main Learning Styles – visual, auditory, kinaesthetic, olfactory and gustatory. But what about the use of intuition? Acceptance of intuition gives us greater access to information, augments the limited perspective of our five familiar senses, and prompts us to transcend our linear view of time and space. Intuition entails listening to the inner voice, and guided journeys provide a means of accessing this resource.

Arnold Mindell refers to 'a world channel' through which communication takes place in ways that cannot always be reduced to the physics of seeing, hearing, moving, touching, smelling or tasting. This offers further evidence for the case to be made for a sixth Learning Style, which is the subject of this book.

So what are guided journeys? Basically, they involve creating pictures in your mind while following a script. Although the form of the 'journey' is controlled by the script, the content remains unpredictable. The process is a means of moving what Carlos Castaneda called 'the assemblage point' and of entering a state of non-ordinary reality. What we call 'reason' is merely a by-product of the habitual position of the assemblage point. Dreaming (and/or visualisation) gives us the fluidity to enter into other worlds and perceive the inconceivable by making the assemblage point shift outside the human domain. It can be argued that the fixation of the assemblage point is so overpowering that it has resulted in us forgetting where we came from and what our purpose was for coming here. Guided visualisation can be seen as a way of reconnecting with what we have forgotten and can be traced back to shamanic practices in pagan times.

A shaman is a person who journeys to non-ordinary reality in an altered state of consciousness. This state can be induced by rhythmic drumming, fasting, spiral dancing or by the use of psychoactive drugs. The purpose of the journey may be to diagnose or treat illnesses, for divination or prophecy, for acquisition of power, to solicit advice or for contact with spirits of the dead. In a sense, whether or not shamanic experience is simply the product of the imagination is irrelevant, as this does not make the process any less real to the participants.

As so-called primitive peoples lacked our advanced level of medical technology, they were motivated to develop the non-technical capacities of the human mind for health and healing. Moreover, the basic uniformity of shamanic methods practised by tribal peoples from Siberia to Australia would suggest that, through trial and error, they arrived at the same conclusions. Perhaps an evolution of human consciousness galvanised by common needs, ideologies, mythologies, or religious intents evoked a collective expression. These ancient methods have been time-tested. In fact, they have been tested immeasurably longer than the other therapies now in vogue. Techniques used by practitioners of NLP – the use of anecdote as metaphor to challenge clients, for example – were used by Native American storytellers enchanting their audiences round the camp fire with their tales of coyote – the trickster. And the use of hypnosis for healing purposes can be traced back to the trance work practised by shamans.

The ancient tradition of shamanism appears to date back to Paleolithic times. Europe has the oldest evidence – animal skulls and bones believed to be shamanic ritual offerings found at sites inhabited between 50,000 and 30,000 BC. The word shaman is derived from a word in the Tungusic language of Siberia, one of the areas in which the classical form of shamanism is found.

Although shamanic practice obviously varies from culture to culture, there are certain core elements that are universal. The shaman traditionally 'journeys' to one of three places – the Lower World, the Middle World or the Upper World. The Lower World is where the shaman 'journeys' to meet Power Animals or Helpers who often have healing powers. The Upper World is where the shaman meets Sacred Teachers who can help with philosophical questions. The Middle World is where the Shaman 'journeys' to see our reality in its non-ordinary reality form. For example, he/she might journey to the Middle World to gain a deeper insight into a relationship he/she has with someone in this reality. There are also shamanic journeys to the Land of the Dead to contact people who have passed on or to help the dying pass on.

The following descriptions of the Upper and Lower Worlds are taken from *Soul Retrieval* by Sandra Ingerman.

> "The Upper World is experienced by some as ethereal. The lighting is often very bright, and the colours can go from blinding light to soft pastels, to grey, to complete darkness. In the Upper World I know that I am standing on something but am often unsure what is holding me there. I might come across a crystalline city with intricate buildings of chambers made of crystal and glass. Or there might be a lake to lie beside, or a city of clouds. Power animals live here, as well as teachers in human form who can offer wise guidance on human relationships.

> "In sharp contrast to the non-corporeal Upper World, the Lower World is reached through a tunnel leading down into the earth. Although non-ordinary beings and occurrences are the rule here, the landscapes are often recognisably earthy: caves, seas, dense jungle, and forests. I can stick my fingers into the earth here. The beings inhabiting the Lower World are the spirits of plants and animals, as well as human spirits who are connected with the mysteries of the earth."

Another form of journeying that is undertaken is known as a Soul Retrieval. It is believed that when one undergoes a traumatic experience such as a major operation, sexual abuse or bereavement, part of the soul leaves the body to escape from the situation. Soul loss, like its psychological counterpart 'disassociation', implies a splitting off of parts of the psyche as a result of trauma. The shaman will journey to find and persuade the lost soul part to return to the client to make the person whole again.

Michael Harner, an American anthropologist, has developed a practical form of core shamanism more appropriate for people living in the twenty-first century. The idea is that instead of turning to a shaman for help with problems, you become your own shamanic practitioner and 'journey' yourself to the different worlds for help or guidance. Michael Harner was responsible for setting up "The Foundation for Shamanic Studies" in the USA. This organisation runs training courses, carries out research, and offers financial support to the few remaining living shamans that can be found in remote regions of the world, to enable them to continue their work and pass on their knowledge to future generations.

Attempts to explain shamans and their cures have been numerous. Some scholars have drawn parallels between shamanistic healing and psychoanalytic cures and have concluded that in both instances therapeutic symbols are created, leading to psychological release and physiological curing. Several anthropologists, rejecting the theory that shamans are basically neurotics or psychotics, have suggested that shamans possess certain cognitive abilities that are distinguishably superior to those of the rest of the community. Other scholars simply explain shamanism as the precursor of a more organised religious system or as a technique for achieving ecstasy. What cannot be disputed, however, is the fact that its practice has withstood the test of time and that reputable psychologists such as Gagan are now incorporating shamanism into their work.

Whether we endorse it or not, shamanism excites our imaginations, resonating with the right side of the brain, where creativity, intuition, spontaneity, and even healing capacities are said to reside. DNA, the macro-molecule that defines life, has within it a natural tendency to trigger spontaneous healing. A vital means for mobilising this tendency is imagery, which is most beneficial when it evokes emotion to energise the image into healing action. Whether the emotion felt is positive or negative seems not to matter; rather it is the intensity of the feeling that gives it power to affect body function.

With 'guided' as opposed to the freer forms of visualisation used in shamanic work, the role of the guide is clearly crucial to ensure a successful outcome. The guide needs to be attentive to the timing of the group and respectful of everyone's experience. His/her role is not to judge but to accept people for who and what they are. What is required is trust in the process and in each person's ability to interpret their own experiences. Because imagery created during the visualisation process originates from within, the participants can usually grasp their implications without any need for intervention by the facilitator.

The unconventional nature of shamanic journeys could be off-putting to certain clients, whereas guided visualisation is more acceptable and has a wider appeal. Moreover, it can be used in a variety of settings – by teachers in classrooms, by trainers in seminars, and by therapists with groups or individual clients. Guided journeys can also be popular with children. They often have imaginary friends they talk to and find it relatively easy to move from one reality into another. Here is a sample script that can be used for this purpose.

Meeting the Inner Friend

Close your eyes and concentrate on your breath moving in ... and ... out ... of your nostrils. And as you continue to breathe in ... and ... out of your nostrils, imagine that you're on a path in a very thick forest. All around you are beautiful green trees, and you walk down this path towards the sound of water. You come to a small stream, and you walk over to the stream and look at your reflection in the water. (Pause)

Soon you feel someone else standing next to you, and you feel completely safe. You see another reflection next to yours in the water – perhaps an old, wise person, an animal, or an imaginary being – someone you feel is your friend, someone you have known a very long time, and someone you know you can trust. Your friend invites to you to follow across a small bridge that crosses the stream. You follow and find yourself climbing a hill that leads to a cave. Your friend enters the cave, sits down, and invites you to follow. You enter the cave and sit down, and your friend begins to tell you about yourself. (Pause one minute.)

You may have a particular question you'd like to ask your friend, and you do that now. You listen carefully to the answer. (Pause one minute.)

Your special friend tells you that you can return to the cave whenever you like. He or she will always be there waiting for you, to help you with anything that you need. You thank your friend, walk back down the path over the bridge, looking once again at your reflection in the water. You notice how you feel as you walk up the path, out of the forest, and become aware of sitting here, fully present. Count to three to yourself, slowly open your eyes and stretch your arms and legs. Welcome back!

People are most receptive to right-brain insights when the body is relaxed and the mind free from internal chatter. Moreover, brain research confirms that as stress increases, the ability to learn decreases so establishing the right kind of atmosphere is clearly crucial. It is suggested that the scripts are read with a musical accompaniment to help produce conducive conditions. You can make use of the Baroque music that Dr Lozanov recommends for the Passive Concert in the Suggestopedic cycle. The beat per second paces the brain into a slower frequency alpha range of 7 to 11 cycles per second.

When words and music are closely associated, both are lodged in the right hemisphere of the brain – where metaphors are understood and emotions realised. A funeral procession would seem incomplete without Chopin's Funeral March or the slow movement of the Eroica. Such emotional reinforcement is required because in our day-to-day lives our deepest feelings become somewhat inaccessible to us. Our highly successful adaptation as a species depends upon our being able to suppress or repress immediate emotional responses. Music can also bring groups of people together. Anyone who has played in an orchestra or sung in a choir knows that the process helps to facilitate group feelings of togetherness.

You will find that affirmations have been built into the scripts for visualisation or included in the form of poems and chants. Our world is full of affirmations – "Have a good day" or "Enjoy your holidays", for example. We affirm because we like to wish the best for others and an affirmation 'makes firm' the things we want. It is a suggestion, a prediction, a blessing and well-wishing. And the more we affirm goodness in others, the more likely we are to find it.

Affirmations can be described as 'brain convincers' as they can be used to counter the little voice which comes with limiting self-beliefs. They can confuse and contradict our internal belief systems and displace negative and limiting attitudes with more positive ones. A changed image can lead to a changed behaviour and this is why affirmations can be such a powerful tool. The way the process works is explained in the following quote taken from *Higher Creativity* by Harman and Rheingold.

> "Since the mind also operates by the process of infer-ence, the mere creation of a mental image, similar to the real object, will cause it to react as if faced by the actuality. The image of an imagined object has mental effects that are in some ways very similar to the image of an object that is actually perceived…. If one is able to imagine something to be true, part of the mind appears to accept that imagined outcome as reality."

It has been established that positive reinforcement and carefully chosen words can actually change the structure of the brain. An amine called serotonin plays a critical role in self-esteem. When there is immediate positive reinforcement, serotonin is released simultaneously into the brain and intestines inducing a sense of well-being and security. This feeling coincides with the chemical conditions for enhanced neural networking and higher order thinking.

It should be pointed out that not everyone will be willing to share their experiences in a group, especially if they are relatively new arrivals. If this turns out to be the case, there is clearly no point in forcing them to do so. As a follow-up to the visualisation, the participants can be invited to produce a piece of creative writing based on their experiences. Those members of the group who were reluctant to share their journeys with their fellow group members will probably feel more at ease when it comes to writing about them and in this way they will have the opportunity to take part in the process. Other forms of follow-up work could include drawing, painting, dancing, or singing. Expressing and communicating are ways of imprinting the information in our memories so it is helpful to follow imagery work with a verbal and/or non-verbal mode of expressing what we have experienced.

As a result of recently acquired knowledge of how the brain works, we now know that an experience with a powerful attachment to emotions or feelings is more likely to be retained in the long-term memory. By inviting the learners to attune to their feelings during visualisation, we can ensure this has a better chance of taking place.

If any of the participants seem to be a bit 'spaced out' after a guided visualisation, holding the neuro-vascular points on the forehead (the emotional stress release points halfway between the eyebrows and the hairline) will stimulate the flow of blood to the front part of the brain. This will activate the area of the brain that we use when making decisions, away from the back brain which relies on old memories and past experiences, thus helping the subject to regain control. If difficulty is experienced in finding these points, placing the fingertips of both hands on the centre of the forehead and simply massaging from the centre to the sides, can also have a beneficial effect.

A number of factors contribute to the way in which an individual approaches learning experiences including environmental, emotional, sociological, physical and psychological. The visualisation presented below can be used to stimulate participants into thinking about their preferred patterns of learning. It is taken from *Accelerated Learning in the Classroom* by Alistair Smith:

> *"As you listen to the music, I'd like you to relax. Feel the soles of your feet on the floor, settle down and prepare to enjoy a journey. You may close your eyes if you wish. Breathe deeply. As you listen to the music, relax from the top of your head to the soles of your feet. Enjoy the feeling.*
>
> *"... Pause ... We are about to begin a journey to explore how you enjoy learning best. When we return you'll know all*

you need to know to help you begin to learn successfully.... Pause ... As you relax your eyes and your mouth and your ears and your neck, continue to breathe deeply and enjoy the music.

"Take yourself to a place where you enjoy learning. Enjoy the sights and sounds of being there. As you continue to relax and listen to the music, enjoy the sounds as you learn successfully. Whether your place is light or dark or warm or cool, you can feel success as a learner when you are there. When you are being even more successful as a learner enjoy the experience, continue to relax, asking yourself 'What is it that is making me so successful here? Is the learning fun? What is making it fun? Is it useful? In what ways is it useful?' ... Pause ... As you continue to relax and see and hear and feel yourself being a successful learner, how are others helping you be successful? Breathe deeply, listen to the music ... And as you enjoy being in your perfect learning place, ask yourself 'What's the best time of day for me to be learning?'

"As you enjoy the music and continue to breathe deeply you may like to think a little more about how you learn best ... what sort of things do you enjoy doing as you learn? Think of the subject you learn best. What is it you do in that subject that helps you more than anything else? And as you continue to breathe deeply, enjoying the music and your successes in learning spend some time there ... Pause ... before preparing to come back with all the secrets of your learning successes. And as the music fades and my voice rises, be aware of being back here (in the classroom) and of the others around you. Gently stretch out as the music stops."

As well as there being different Learning Styles, there are also Intelligence Types to consider. Howard Gardner, an educational psychologist at Harvard University, has gathered evidence to suggest that there are at least eight different types – linguistic, mathematical, spatial, bodily-kinaesthetic, musical, interpersonal – the way we relate to others, intrapersonal – our talent to self-evaluate, and naturalist – our ability to classify and categorise.

Boys, being later developers linguistically, grow up with an emphasis on doing rather than talking. The result is that they tend to have an underdeveloped interpersonal ability. It is often the case that they are discouraged from discussing or being open about feelings, and their world is more likely to be hierarchical, action-focused and competitive. Guided visualisations using relaxation techniques to appropriate music can help to develop interpersonal intelligence in such cases.

Our fast-paced, time-segmented daily lives make it difficult to be fully present at any one moment. We're always thinking about what's going to happen next and there is no time for quiet or reflection. The use of guided visualisation enables us to step outside this web we weave ourselves into and to reconnect with our inner resources.

The scripts for the visualisations in the main core of this work are mainly based on myths and folk tales. These provide an ideal source of material as they include archetypal figures we can all relate to, and tap into the collective unconscious. (In Jungian theory, this is the part of the unconscious mind which is inherited and contains universal thought patterns and memories.) Jung stressed that an image from the unconscious simply acknowledged is often what sets in motion a healing process. In many mystery rites, appropriate conditions were created which produced a powerful vision for the participants. The vision was then incubated and provided a rich source for creative work. This can be one of the therapeutic effects of using guided imagery.

This book intentionally sticks to basically the same format for each journey to establish a 'ritual' or formula that participants can get accustomed to so as to increase their sense of security in the process. This is a personal choice and you may prefer to include more variety. There are plenty of alternative models to choose from and these can be found in the books listed in the bibliography.

The samples of creative writing below were produced after a guided journey to Avalon – the Celtic paradise. (The script for this visualization can be found in *A Multiple Intelligences Road To An ELT Classroom*.) The poem was written by a Ukrainian teacher of

English in response to her first experience of the technique at an IATEFL (International Association of Teachers of English as a Foreign Language) Conference called "Grammar In Action" in Kyiv.

A silver-haired witch in her flowing robe
Who may even take you around the globe
Loneliness and quietness everywhere around me
Mist coming in waves and awaiting what is should be
The icy touch of crystal clear water of the lake
And the immense desire, nothing to break
Bliss and apprehension of mysteries driving fore and fore
And a soft soothing voice you'd like to hear more and more.
— N. Filippova, Kyiv — Ukraine, 22/11/96

Next is a fragment from another account of a journey to Avalon written by a native speaker of English from Wimborne in Dorset.

Morgana came to take me to Avalon. She was dressed in long purple and green robes, with a sash across her left shoulder. She was wearing a gold crown. I found it very hard though to bring her face into focus, as though a mist surrounded her features. At times her face was almost heart-shaped, with her sleek black hair held back tightly beneath the crown. At other times, her hair was long and blonde, loosely dropping each side of her face. Both these personages were young; one severely, the other softly, beautiful. Then both would give way to a third face — that of an old witch-like character, with untidy grey hair....

When we arrived at the pool, Morgana indicated that I should enter the water, in order to refresh myself physically and spiritually. The water was golden and opaque. As I entered, I felt the waters dissolving my body, until, with only my head above the water's surface, only my head remained. Morgana suggested I should find some object that I could take back as a keepsake. But I had only a head; no arms or hands to lay hold of such an object.

I dropped my head under the water. Luckily it did not disappear, as the rest of my body had, but turned into a form of flatfish with golden and orange scales. Thus transformed I swam to the bottom of the pool, meaning to look for some kind of shell. None pleased me — but then J saw, almost buried in the sand at the pool's base, a purple bauble, more or less the size of a ping-pong ball. J was able to suck it into my mouth and held it in that way as J swam back to the pool's surface. Morgana was there waiting for me. She said it was now time to leave Avalon. As J rose out of the water, my body came back to me. J was utterly refreshed. J retrieved the purple bauble from my mouth and carried it in my hand as we set off away from Avalon back across the water.

It is interesting to note that shape-shifting, taking on another form or body as described in the account above, is a common occurrence on journeys in a trance state.

Another way of using visualisation is to energise something you plan to do in a trance state before trying it out. By attacking any fears you have in non-ordinary reality first, they become easier to manage in this reality. Moreover, by visualising an intended undertaking with a successful outcome, you are more likely to approach it with self-assurance and in balance. This process parallels what top sports people do before competing in events. Empirical studies indicate that imagery rehearsal has a definite influence on behaviour and that mental imaging impacts on real-life situations. Such effects have been noted in the sphere of physical performance, where research reveals that mental practice as an adjunct to physical practice can enhance athletic skills. To find out more about how the technique can be used in sports, refer to *The Inner Game of Tennis* by W. Timothy Gallwey. There are also two sequels called *The Inner Game of Skiing* and *The Inner Game of Golf*.

When you are feeling down and have no one to turn to, there remains one place you can always go – to your teachers in non-ordinary reality or, if you prefer the terminology, to the resources to be found within – your inner voice. Whether you believe in the power of intuition, or helpers in other realities, is not really important. What matters is that it works! It was Jung who said that "the more stubbornly we believe that all increase has to come from without, the greater becomes our inner poverty". This can be taken one stage further. For if we believe that all increase has to come from without, the greater becomes our inability to tap into our own source of power for healing purposes. The only way *The*

Power of Metaphor can be considered to be successful is if it empowers the people who use it and their clients.

It is clear that the combination of story telling leading into guided visualisation to facilitate the healing power of metaphor can prove to be beneficial in a wide variety of settings. It is hoped that the sample scripts presented in the book and the appendix on how to formulate your own scripts will prove to be useful for you in your own field of work and/or for your own personal development.

> "Stories are medicine…. They have such power; they do not require that we do, be, act anything – we need only listen. The remedies for repair or reclamation of any lost psychic drive are contained in stories."
> – Clarissa Pinkola Estes

> "Your imagination, your capacity to fantasise or probe the future through pictures in your mind's eye, is one of the greatest resources you have as a human being. You can learn to enjoy and to control the greatest powers of your imagination and from these inner resources you can often forge a better reality."
> – Singer and Switzer,
>   *Mind-Play: The Creative Uses of Fantasy*

> "The essential act of imaging, like all creative art, is the bringing into being of a vision. The images we spin inwardly become the reality we spin out."
> – Maureen Murdock, *Spinning Inward*

> "If you should feel the inner tremble that comes from a mountain-top experience, savour the moment; be aware of the sensations in your body and enjoy them – this is a rare gift from your right brain. The right hemisphere is the mysterious artistic side of the brain where metaphors are understood and emotions are realised. It is where dreams and imagery occur and fantasies are born."
> – Marilee Zdenek, *The Right Brain Experience*

Slaying the Dragon called Fear

[Overcoming the
Barriers to Learning]

All learning is affected by our own personal history; we have a lifetime of experiences, beliefs, values and attitudes about each subject and our ability to learn it. Lozanov, the Bulgarian psychotherapist who developed the Suggestopedic Approach to teaching, calls these biases. He believes that all learning is heavily influenced by all of the biases, and the presenters who influence the biases are much more likely to be successful.

I can still clearly remember my maths teacher in secondary school, for example, more than thirty years ago. Whenever I made a mistake, he would make me stand on one leg facing the wall, holding my tongue between my fingers so the saliva would dribble down my chin. Not surprisingly, this left me with a learning block which has remained with me ever since. It is likely that most of us have similar anecdotes to relate. Experiences like this help to make us into the people we are and perhaps even motivate us into turning to one of the caring professions as a career – not wanting others to suffer the same way that we have.

It is interesting to note that in tribal societies the person chosen to be the shaman or Medicine Man was often a wounded healer – someone who had been through a near-death experience and who was consequently well suited to helping others through difficult times in their lives.

How do we deal with the barriers to learning that result from such wounding? The following story and accompanying visualisation have been designed with this aim in mind.

Giant Steps

Once upon a time, in a land far away, there lived an enormous giant. He was at least ten feet tall, with a mane of red hair and a beard, and in his hand he carried a mighty axe.

Every year, on the same day, at the same time, the giant would walk down from the mountains which were his home, to stand outside the castle walls and terrorise the inhabitants.

"Come, send me your bravest man, and I will fight him," the giant would shout, towering over the wall and waving his axe menacingly. "Send me someone to fight, or I will knock down your castle walls and kill everyone."

And every year, the gate in the castle wall would open slowly and, fearfully, one poor, valiant soul would walk out to face certain death.

"Is this the best you can do?" the giant would laugh mockingly.

The poor wretch would stand, mesmerised by the enormity of the giant and the task in hand. Not one person had even managed to draw his sword, before the giant would crush them with his mighty fist, and chop them into tiny pieces with his axe.

But (and there is always a 'but' in stories like this) one day a young prince arrived in the town. "Why does everyone here look so frightened and sad?" he asked a fellow traveller.

"You haven't seen the giant yet," replied the traveller.

"What giant?"' asked the young prince, intrigued. The traveller told him the tale.

"Every year, on this very day, the giant arrives and challenges our bravest to a duel. And every year, he slays them exactly where they stand. They don't even move or attempt to fight. It's as though the giant hypnotises them."

"We'll see about that," said the young prince.

When the giant arrived later that day, he was waiting for him.

"Send me your bravest man, and I will fight him," the giant shouted.

"I am here," said the young prince, throwing open the gate, and striding out towards him.

For a moment, they stood and faced each other. Although he was still a long way away from him, the young prince was instantly struck by the incredible size and shocking appearance of his opponent. But, summoning up all his courage, he started to walk towards the giant, brandishing his sword, and never taking his eyes off that dreadful face with the red hair and the red beard.

Suddenly, he realised that as he was walking, the giant – rather than appearing larger – actually began to shrink before his very eyes. He stopped and stared. The giant was only five feet tall.

He walked closer to him still, then stopped and stared. Now the giant was only two feet tall. He continued walking until he was face to face with the giant, and with each step he took, he saw the giant shrink. By now the giant was so small, that he looked up at the young prince. He was only twelve inches tall.

The young prince took his sword, and plunged it into the giant's heart. As the giant lay dying on the ground, the young prince bent down and whispered to him, "Who are you? What's your name?"

With his dying breath, the giant replied, "My name is Fear".

– adapted from Margaret Parkin, *Tales for Trainers*

A Guided Visualisation: Slaying the Dragon called Fear

SCRIPT FOR THE GUIDE: (To be read in a gentle trance-inducing voice.) Make yourself comfortable and close your eyes. Take a few deep breaths to help you relax. Feel the tension disappear stage by stage from the top of your head to the tips of your toes. Let your surroundings fade away as you gradually sink backwards through time and actuality and pass through the gateway of reality into the dreamtime. (When the participants are fully relaxed, begin the next stage.)

All your life you've been a coward. Just stop for a moment to consider what that means. All your life you've taken the easy way out, running away from danger instead of facing up to your fears. Just stop for a moment to consider all the opportunities you've missed by not having the courage to step into the unknown. You have a minute of clock time, equal to all the time you need, to reflect on all the chances you've let slip through your fingers over the years....

The time has now come to leave the past behind you. Today's a very special day in your life, the day you choose to take a different path, the day you finally face up to and overcome your fears, the day you find your courage and become the person you were born to be, the day you take control of your life again.

You find yourself walking along a pathway. The stars and the full moon light your way through the darkness and guide you towards your goal. Your destination is the entrance to a cave that lies straight ahead of you, the cave where the dragon called Fear lies in wait. But with each step you take, your determination to succeed in your mission grows. And with each step you take your self-belief and confidence grow for you know that nothing can stand in your way. You've waited too long for this moment to throw it all away by letting your fear get the better of you again. You have a minute of clock time, equal to all the time you need, to see the sky-blue flame of intent grow inside you, the sky-blue flame of intent that can never be extinguished, and let it fill you with all the power you could ever need, the power that will enable you to dance your dreams awake, the power that will enable you to cross the rainbow bridge....

And now you find yourself face to face with the dragon and the opportunity to become the master of your life again instead of a pitiable victim of circumstance. Let the sky-blue flame expand inside you until it reaches out to encompass all that is, all that has been, and all that will be and consumes the dragon, the obstacle that stands in the way of your heart's content and happiness, the obstacle that has never been anything more than just a figment of your imagination. Now enter the mouth of the cave where a mirror awaits you. In this mirror you can see whoever you want to see and be whoever you want to be. And you have a minute of clock time, equal to all the time you need, to appreciate the new person now standing before you, the person you were always born to be....

Now the time has come for you to return, not as the person you were before but as the person you were always born to be, the master of your own destiny. And as you leave the cave behind you and walk back along the path, make sure you hold on to the precious gift you've been given so you can put it to good use the other side of the gateway. And with each step you take you leave the dreamtime behind, as the new you returns along the pathway, back, back, the same way you came, back to the place you started from. Welcome home!

Open your eyes now and stretch your arms and legs. Take a few minutes in silence to make some notes on the experience you had on your journeys, which you can then share with the rest of the group/make a note of in your dream journal.

The following story has been included as it presents a picture of what can be accomplished once the dragon called fear has been slain. It is an adaptation of a traditional British folk tale called *The Dauntless Girl*. Once you have done away with your Dragon, everything becomes possible and there is no limit to what you can achieve.

The Girl who was Frightened of Nothing

"Damn it!" said the farmer. "Not a drop left."

"Not one?" asked the blacksmith, raising his glass and inspecting it. His last inch of whisky glowed like molten honey in the flickering firelight.

"Why not?" said the miller.

"You fool!" said the farmer. "Because the bottle's empty." He peered into the flames. "Never mind that though," he said. "We'll send out my Mary. She'll go down to the inn and bring us another bottle."

"What?" said the blacksmith. "She'll be afraid to go out on such a dark night, all the way down to the village, and all on her own."

"Never!" said the farmer. "She's afraid of nothing — nothing live or dead. She's worth all my lads put together."

The farmer gave a shout and Mary came out of the kitchen. She stood and she listened. She went out into the dark night and in a little time returned with another bottle of whisky.

The miller and the blacksmith were delighted. They drank to her health, but later the miller said, "That's a strange thing, though."

"What's that?" asked the farmer.

"That she should be so bold, your Mary."

"Bold as brass," said the blacksmith. "Out and alone and the night so dark."

"That's nothing at all," said the farmer. "She'd go anywhere, day or night. She's afraid of nothing — nothing live or dead."

"Words," said the blacksmith. "But my, this whisky tastes good."

"Words nothing," said the farmer. "I bet you a golden guinea that neither of you can name anything that girl will not do."

The miller scratched his head and the blacksmith peered at the golden guinea of whisky in his glass. "All right," said the blacksmith. "Let's meet here again at the same time next week. Then I'll name something Mary will not do."

Next week the blacksmith went to see the priest and borrowed the key of the church door from him. Then he paid a visit to the sexton and showed him the key.

"What do you want with that?" asked the sexton.

"What I want with you," said the blacksmith, "is this. I want you to go into the church tonight, just before midnight, and hide yourself in the dead house."

"Never," said the sexton.

"Not for half a guinea?" asked the blacksmith.

The old sexton's eyes popped out of his head. "That's a different matter!" he said. "But what's all this for then?"

"To frighten that brazen farm girl, Mary," said the blacksmith, grinning. "When she comes to the dead house, just give a moan or a holler."

The old sexton's desire for half the guinea was even greater than his fear. He hummed and hawed and at last agreed to do as the black-smith asked.

Then the blacksmith clumped the sexton on the back with his massive fist and the old sexton coughed. "I'll see you tomorrow," said the blacksmith, "and settle the account. Just before midnight, then! Not a minute later!"

The sexton nodded and the blacksmith strode up to the farm. Darkness was falling and the farmer and the miller were already drinking and waiting for him.

"Well," said the farmer. "Are you or aren't you?"

"This," said the blacksmith, "is what your Mary will not do. She won't go into the church alone at midnight...."

"No," said the miller.

"... and go to the dead house," continued the blacksmith, "and bring back a skull bone. That's what she won't do."

"Never," said the miller.

The farmer gave a shout and Mary came out of the kitchen. She stood and listened; and later, at midnight, she went out into the darkness and walked down to the church.

Mary opened the church door. She held up her lamp and clattered down the steps to the dead house. She pushed open its creaking door and saw skulls and thigh bones and bones of every kind gleaming in front of her. She stooped and picked up the nearest skull bone.

"Let that be," moaned a muffled voice from behind the dead house door. "That's my mother's skull bone."

So Mary put that skull down and picked up another.

"Let that be," moaned a muffled voice from behind the dead house door. "That's my father's skull bone."

So Mary put that skull bone down too and picked up yet another one. And, as she did so, she angrily called out, "Father or mother, sister or brother, J must have a skull bone and that's my last word." Then she walked out of the dead house, slammed the door, and hurried up the steps and back up to the farm.

Mary put the skull bone on the table in front of the farmer. "There's your skull bone, master," she said, and started off for the kitchen.

"Wait a minute!" said the farmer, grinning and shivering at one and the same time. "Didn't you hear anything in the dead house, Mary?"

"Yes," she said. "Some fool of a ghost called out to me: 'Let that be! That's my mother's skull bone' and 'Let that be! That's my father's skull bone.' But J told him straight; 'Father or mother, sister or brother, J must have a skull bone.'"

The miller and the blacksmith stared at Mary and shook their heads.

"So J took one," said Mary, "and here J am and here it is." She looked down at the three faces flickering in the firelight. "As J was going away," she said, "after J had locked the door, J heard the old ghost hollering and shrieking like mad."

The blacksmith and the miller looked at each other and got to their feet.

"That'll do then, Mary," said the farmer.

The blacksmith knew that the sexton must have been scared out of his wits at being locked all alone in the dead house. They all raced down to the church, and clattered down the steps into the dead house, but they were too late. They found the old sexton lying stone dead on his face.

"That's what comes of trying to frighten a poor young girl," said the farmer. So the blacksmith gave the farmer a golden guinea and the farmer gave it to his Mary.

Mary and her daring were known in every house. And after her visit to the dead house, and the death of the old sexton, her fame spread for miles and miles around.

One day the squire, who lived three villages off, rode up to the farm and asked the farmer if he could talk to Mary.

"I've heard," said the squire, "that you're afraid of nothing." Mary nodded.

"Nothing live or dead," said the farmer proudly.

"Listen then!" said the squire. "Last year my old mother died and was buried. But she will not rest. She keeps coming back into the house, and especially at mealtimes. Sometimes you can see her, sometimes you can't. And when you can't, you can still see a knife and fork get up off the table and play about where her hands would be."

"That's a strange thing altogether," said the farmer, "that she should go on walking."

"Strange and unnatural," said the squire. "And now my servants won't stay with me, not one of them. They're all afraid of her."

The farmer sighed and shook his head. "Hard to come by, good servants," he said.

"So," said the squire, "seeing as she's afraid of nothing, nothing live or dead, I'd like to ask your girl to come and work with me."

Mary was pleased at the prospect of such good employment and, sorry as he was to lose her, the farmer saw there was nothing for it but to let her go.

"I'll come," said the girl. "I'm not afraid of ghosts. But you ought to take account of that in my wages."

"I will," said the squire.

So Mary went back with the squire to be his servant. The first thing she always did was to lay a place for the ghost at the table, and she took great care not to let the knife and fork criss-cross.

At meals, Mary passed the ghost the meat and vegetables and sauce and gravy. And then she said: "Pepper, madam?" and "Salt, madam?" The ghost of the squire's mother was pleased enough. Things went on the same from day to day until the squire had to go up to London to settle some legal business.

Next morning, Mary was down on her knees, cleaning the parlour grate, when she noticed something thin and glimmering push in through the parlour door, which was just ajar; when it got inside the room, the shape began to swell and open out. It was the old ghost.

For the first time, the ghost spoke to the girl. "Mary," she said in a hollow voice, "are you afraid of me?"

"No, madam," said Mary. "I've no cause to be afraid of you, for you are dead and I'm alive."

For a while the ghost looked at the girl kneeling by the parlour grate. "Mary," she said, "will you come down into the cellar with me? You mustn't bring a light – but I'll shine enough to light the way for you."

So the two of them went down the cellar steps and the ghost shone like an old lantern. When they got down to the bottom, they went down a passage, and took a right turn and a left, and then the ghost pointed to some loose tiles in one corner. "Pick up those tiles," she said.

Mary did as she was asked. And underneath the tiles were two bags of gold, a big one and a little one.

The ghost quivered. "Mary," she said, "that big bag is for your master. But the little bag is for you, for you are a dauntless girl and deserve it."

Before Mary could open the bag or even open her mouth, the old ghost drifted up the steps and out of sight. She was never seen again and Mary had a devil of a time groping her way along the dark passage and up out of the cellar.

After three days, the squire came back from London.

"Good morning, Mary," he said. "Have you seen anything of my mother while I've been away?"

"Yes, sir," said Mary. "That I have." She opened her eyes wide. "And if you aren't afraid of coming down into the cellar with me, I'll show you something."

The squire laughed. "I'm not afraid, if you're not afraid," he said, for the dauntless girl was a very pretty girl. So Mary lit a candle and led the squire down into the cellar, walked along the passage, took a right turn and a left, and raised the loose tiles in the corner for a second time.

"Two bags," said the squire.

"Two bags of gold," said Mary. "The little one is for you and the big one is for me."

"Well I never!" said the squire, and he said nothing else. He did think that his mother might have given him the big bag, as indeed she had, but all the same he took what he could.

After that, Mary always crossed the knives and forks at mealtimes to prevent the old ghost from telling what she had done.

The squire thought things over: the gold and the ghost and Mary's good looks. What with one thing and another he proposed to Mary, and the dauntless girl, she accepted him. In a little while they married, and so the squire did get both bags of gold after all.

– adapted from Kevin Crossley-Holland, *British Folk Tales*

Power Shield Prayer

I am strength and the strength is strong.
Strong is my power
My power protects me.
I see the power around me.
From inside it comes to encircle me in its light
The light I see is shining like the sun.
I am strength and the strength is strong.
Strong is my power.
My power protects me.
— Mary Summer Rain, *Ancient Echoes*

Activities for Trainers

Most of us are experts at putting ourselves down and the people we work with are no exception. Here is an activity designed to help reverse the process – to help people build themselves up.

"Everybody stand up please. I'm going to read out a list of adjectives and I'd like you to sit down when you hear an adjective that describes the way you're feeling." (If anyone is still standing when you come to the end of your list, then ask them to produce an adjective of their own. Notice how only positive adjectives have been included.)

deserving	unique	creative
supportive	clever	responsible
flexible	active	enthusiastic
thoughtful	light-hearted	confident
likeable	responsive	loveable
exciting	self-aware	happy
intelligent	sensitive	interesting
tactful	artistic	tolerant
perceptive	kind	modest

Simple *re-framing* exercises can be used to discourage limiting beliefs. "I'm no good at ..." statements can be challenged with What would it be like if you were good at...? It can also be helpful to encourage outcome thinking – If you were to be successful, what would it be like? What would others see you doing? What would others be saying to you and how would you feel about it?

Another technique that can be employed is to encourage distancing from the belief – How would you help others to be good at…? What three tips would you give someone who wanted to be good at…?

Reformulation, a technique taken from NLP, can also be a helpful device for promoting self-esteem.

Make a list of all of the things you think you should do. Give yourself a ten-minute time limit. Now reformulate the items in your list by using the following wording: If I really wanted to I could….

You will probably find some things now seem much more possible and there are other things which you now want to abandon. This is what Louise Hay has to say about the modal should: "… I believe that 'should' is one of the most damaging words in our language. Every time we use should we are in effect saying 'wrong'. Either we are wrong or we were wrong or we are going to be wrong. I don't think we need more wrongs in our life. We need more freedom of choice. I would like to take the word SHOULD and remove it from the vocabulary forever. I replace it with the word COULD. Could gives us choice and we are never wrong."

Similarly, you can make a list of all the things you can't do, then add the word *yet* to the end of each. Alternatively, the ideas can be reformulated using the structure I can learn how to … if I want/choose to.

When working with groups, the original lists can be burnt in a fire ceremony or thrown into a wastepaper bin to make the process more powerful. Alternatively, the participants might prefer to devise a disposal ceremony of their own making.

The Eagle's Gift

[Rising above
Self-imposed Limitations]

Shamanic experience for initiates is often so powerful that the participant's response to the process can be extreme. In the story that follows, Sheila's initial response takes this form. However, upon reflection and after sharing her thoughts with her friend, she eventually comes to a more practical understanding of how to put what she has learned into practice. The story helps to show how what we learn in non-ordinary reality can be made use of in our everyday lives. Jung wrote that "the more stubbornly we believe that all increase has to come from within, the greater becomes our inner poverty". *The Eagle's Flight* is all about rising above such self-imposed limitations. Native Americans call to the Eagle for vision and enlightenment, and the visualisation that follows the story provides an opportunity for shape-shifting so as to experience the Eagle's vision first hand.

The Eagle's Flight

The great eagle flew high and far, searching for its prey, through mountainous valleys and above wide forests, disdainful of populated areas, keeping only to the wild places where humans seldom ventured.

Then, down it went, rushing from the high sky like a missile to clutch at the fleeing rabbit as the little creature realised too late that its days had ended.

Up flew the eagle, back again to the heights, leisurely flapping its great wings in lazy power, clutching its meal as it returned to its mountain nest.

The speed of the drumming increased. Sheila reluctantly realised that it was time to return to normal consciousness – the shamanic journey was over. She waited for the instructor to tell them to open their eyes, get up from the floor and return to their seats.

The first two evenings not much had happened during the shamanic visualisations but this week she had been that extraordinary bird. She had experienced its enormous freedom and glorious solitude.

Sheila was reluctant to share her experience with the others when the group had reassembled and simply said, "Not much, just a glimpse or two of a bird," when asked what she had seen on her journey. The instructor looked at her curiously but passed on to the next person.

Her friend, Alison, who had brought her to the group meeting three weeks ago, talked at length to the others about her meeting with a dolphin. The instructor explained that a dolphin was one of Alison's power animals and had special qualities that Alison needed to incorporate into her life.

Sheila listened with only half an ear. She had actually been that eagle. Did this mean that the eagle had qualities that she should bring to her life?

After a cup of tea, the group of about fifteen people disbanded and Sheila made her way to the school car park having declined Alison's invitation to go for a drink. Alison was a good friend. They had been working in the same office for years and Alison was always inviting Sheila to some new therapy or teaching. One term it was yoga, another term it was reflexology. This term, Alison had chosen "A beginner's guide to shamanism : practical and powerful ways to change your life for the better". This evening had been the most interesting of all.

Sheila's thoughts were interrupted by the horrible realisation that her car lights were still on and sure enough, when she turned the ignition key, the battery was flat and the engine wouldn't turn. "Damn it !" She decided to walk home. It would take about twenty minutes but she could do with the time by herself before getting home to Bryan, her husband, who would expect her to make some supper and to listen to his interminable story of his day at the office.

It was a cold and dark October evening so Sheila buttoned up her warm blue coat, pulled up her collar and started her walk home through the suburbs. She came to a main road where a large group of youths were congregated noisily in front of a supermarket, leaving no room on the pavement for anyone to pass. Normally, Sheila would have crossed the road but today she continued walking, right through the throng who moved aside as she glided along the pavement.

Her pace quickened. A large cat noticed her and fled. Sheila felt strong and free. Her senses were sharper. She was not afraid.

She arrived home in hardly more than ten minutes and let herself in. Bryan was there, waiting.

"I didn't hear the car," he said.

"No, I left it at the school," she answered. "The battery was flat. I'll attend to it tomorrow."

"How will you get to work tomorrow?" he asked.

"Bus, I suppose," she said, not wanting Bryan to fuss.

Bryan didn't enquire further about the car but changed the subject. "Shall we have some supper now?"

"No, I'm alright, thank you," said Sheila, "I ate only three hours ago."

Bryan felt bemused and annoyed. "So, will you cook me something?" he asked.

"No," said Sheila. "You are not my chick, you know."

Bryan was really angry now. "Look," he said, "I don't know what you've been filling your head with at your evening class, but I'm your husband. I do my jobs around the house and you do yours. Cooking supper is one of your jobs."

"Not any more," answered Sheila calmly, casting him a piercing look.

"Well, I'll make my own," he said, "but next time you want the grass cut or your car serviced, don't look at me."

"I don't need anything from you," said Sheila. "From now on I'm going to fly alone."

"What's got into you?" asked Bryan. "Flying alone? What do think you are? A bird? A plane? Superwoman?"

"I'm an eagle, Bryan, and you are a rabbit. Find a burrow of your own, bunny."

"You've gone mad !" shouted Bryan. "You need a psychiatrist, or a vet!"

"J'm sorry Bryan, J really am," answered Sheila quietly, but seriously, "J want to be free. J didn't realise that before this evening. Not just free of you but free of all the habits and people that J never really chose. J'm sorry. J'll pack some things and J'll go. J'll be in touch."

"But where will you stay tonight?" asked Bryan, concerned.

"J'll find somewhere," she said. "Somewhere right out of town, as far away as J can get."

"Shall J pack you some food?" Bryan asked.

"No thanks," said Sheila, "J'll find what J want when J get hungry."

Sheila walked out of the house, closed the door behind her and disappeared into the night. She walked and walked, getting as far away from the town as possible. This was ridiculous but she was determined to see it through. But it got colder and darker and Sheila found herself getting hungrier too. Where could she go? Who could she talk to? Of course! Alison would understand. Sheila found a phone box and rang Alison.

"Alison, it's Sheila. J'm sorry to ring so late but J've been a bit silly. J had a row and walked out on Bryan and J can't bear to eat humble pie and go home tonight. J couldn't come and stay with you, could J?" she asked.

"Of course you can. Just come round right now. J'll make up a bed in the spare room." said Alison.

Sheila found a taxi and went round to Alison's. "J really appreciate this," she said as Alison opened the door. Alison showed her into the living-room of her townhouse, and there was an opened bottle of wine and two glasses.

"J feel so stupid," said Sheila after she had explained things. J felt so sure J was right to leave home and now J feel such an idiot. All because of that stupid so-called journey when J seemed to become an eagle!"

"I know how you feel," said Alison. "Those journeys are so real and vivid and they can make real life seem drab, can't they?"

"Yes, that's right, so what's the answer?" asked Sheila.

"I don't know," said Alison, "Just plugging away at trying to change life little by little, I suppose."

"Will your dolphin make any difference to you?" asked Sheila.

"Yes, it will," said Alison forcibly, "because I want it to, but it doesn't mean that I'm going to sell my flat, buy a yacht and sail away for the rest of my life."

"What will it mean then, in practical terms?" asked Sheila.

"It will mean that I will make an effort to be freer, more loving and more playful," Alison answered, smiling. "And what will the eagle mean for you?"

"I don't know," said Sheila slowly. "But it will make a difference. Somehow."

"Let's drink to eagles and dolphins," said Alison picking up her glass.

"Yes," agreed Sheila, "To eagles and dolphins."

Notes For Teachers

Pre-listening: A brainstorming session: What qualities do you associate with eagles? Pin up a picture of an eagle on the board and invite the learners to surround it with suitable adjectives to describe their qualities.

Post-listening: Have you ever had an experience like Sheila's that completely changed your life? Tell me about it. How do you think Sheila's life will change in the future? Working in small groups, write a sequel to the story entitled "Sheila's New Life" While this is taking place, you can circulate to provide any assistance required. Each group can then choose a spokesperson to read out their story to the rest of the class.

A Guided Visualisation: The Eagle's Gift

SCRIPT FOR THE GUIDE: (To be read in a gentle trance-inducing voice.) Make yourself comfortable and close your eyes. Take a few deep breaths to help you relax. Feel the tension disappear stage by stage from the top of your head to the tips of your toes. Let your surroundings fade away as you gradually sink backwards through time and actuality and pass through the gateway of reality into the dreamtime. (When the participants are fully relaxed, begin the next stage.)

You find yourself climbing up a steep cliff, fighting against the wind blowing against you. Feel the icy blasts of the wind, taste the salt of the sea on your lips, and hear the cry of the seagulls flying overhead. To make yourself lighter, you need to offload all the emotional baggage you're carrying with you. So gradually, piece by piece, you discard the packages weighing you down and leave them all behind you. And with each weight you take off your back you feel lighter. And so the climb becomes easier until eventually you reach the top. Take a minute of clock time, equal to all the time you need, to appreciate what you have achieved, to say goodbye to what you have left behind you, to give thanks for what you have learnt from those experiences. As this happens, you will feel the eagle's feather brush against you to affirm the new identity you're about to take on…. (The guide and/or an assistant can pass among the participants with a feather at this point.)

Now, as you stand on the clifftop, you can look forward to all the new challenges that lie ahead. And as you look down on the future prospects that await you, feel the wings starting to sprout from your shoulders. With your physical body, you can begin to make the movement of wings with your arms. You also become aware of your eagle eyes. And with each movement of your wings, your sharp eagle eyes grow more acute. And you can see through whatever you gaze upon. Now the wind is blowing from behind you. You wait for a favourable gust and take off. Higher and higher you climb with effortless ease, carried by the currents of air, king of all you survey. This is the moment you were born for. Soaring higher and higher, your eagle body carries you inland, following the course of the river. Take a minute of clock time, equal to all the time you need, to appreciate your new-found sense of freedom….

The water in the river below you sparkles in the sunlight and catches your attention. You swoop down to take a closer look. You see that the banks are lined with all the demons that have plagued you in the past but you refuse to let your fear get the better of you. And when the demons see you coming, they all crawl away for they know that now you're in power and that nothing and nobody can stop you from reaching your goal.

You land on the surface to quench your thirst with the revitalising substance of the life-force. And the crystal clear water rewards you with the gift of clarity. Take a minute of clock time, equal to all the time you need, to appreciate this new-found clarity of vision and your inner eye will show you the future path to take on the next stage of your journey through life....

Now that you've had the opportunity to experience the potential that lies within you, the potential you can draw on, the time has come to shift back into your everyday form and to return to your starting point, the time and the actuality you left behind. And as I start counting slowly from one to ten, you will gradually return to consciousness with a feeling of new-found power and a clear vision of the future path to take. 1 – 2 – 3 – 4 – 5 – 6 – 7 – 8 – 9 – 10 – Welcome back!

Open your eyes now and stretch your arms and legs. Take a few minutes in silence to make some notes on the experiences you had, which you can then share with the rest of the group/make a note of in your dream journal.

Eagle Calling Song

Wingeð One. Sky Spirit.
Hear my call.
Hear my voice.
Come, Wingeð One.
Come to share your
Sky with me.

Sky Spirit. Wingeð One.
See my spirit.
See my heart.
Come to share your
Soul with me.
— *Mary Summer Rain*, Ancient Echoes

Fly like an eagle
Fly so high
Circling the Universe
On wings of pure light
— Native American chant

When we decide to make fundamental changes to our lives, what about the people we leave behind us – like Sheila's husband in *The Eagle's Flight*, for example? If they truly love us, then they can surely appreciate the happiness we find and this can be illustrated by the Aboriginal tale that follows. There is no need to regard following our dreams as a selfish activity as it can bring joy to the significant others in our lives and it is a mark of the way in which we value and honour ourselves.

The First Brolga

In the long ago Dreamtime there was a pretty, very graceful girl called Brolga. She belonged to a group who lived in the northern plains. It was usual then, in this group and most others, for the men to do most of the dancing while the women watched and clapped the beat.

Brolga was different. She could not just sit and watch. She had to dance, and her dancing was special – it had to be seen to be believed. Not only did she perform the traditional dances very well, but she was for ever creating new dances. The men and women of her group loved to watch her, and they constantly talked about her dancing. Her fame spread far and wide, and people from other groups came to watch her as well.

There were many men who wanted to marry Brolga for her beauty and her special talent. But Brolga did not wish to marry anyone.

"I want to be free," she said. " Free to dance in the morning light and free to dance under the stars at night. I must be free to dance and dance and dance. I can never marry."

The men she refused were disappointed; but just as they were drawn to her unusual gift, they also understood how important it was to her, and so they left her alone to dance as she wished.

They all left her alone, that is, except for one. He was a mean man who had caused a lot of trouble in the camp; and he had learned evil magic. Everyone else in the group was afraid of him, and they warned Brolga to be careful.

"He may try to harm you," they whispered, "so stay close to camp where we can guard you."

Brolga listened and promised; and for a time she was very careful. But one spring morning when the sun shone warmly and the wild flowers nodded in the breeze, Brolga forgot her caution and let the dance lead her far, far away from the camp. The temptation was just too great and the world was so beautiful that she wanted to see it all. As the hours passed she danced on and on, getting further and further away from the camp.

Suddenly, and it seemed to come from nowhere, there was a fierce whirlwind in the sky. It howled as it savagely beat against the girl, and the earth trembled where she stood. The evil man had created this whirlwind by magic, and he was there in the centre of it.

"If you will not marry me, you shall not marry anyone," he screamed over the howling wind.

Brolga recognised him immediately and stood still and silent, trying desperately to think of a way to escape.

And then in a flash everything changed. The whirlwind disappeared, and Brolga found that she was no longer a beautiful young girl. Instead of arms she had long, light-boned wings with silvery feathers, and her body was draped in grey softness.

For a moment she felt desperately sad; but immediately to her delight she discovered that even as a bird she could still dance. Discovering at every moment more of the powers and elegance of her new body, she danced and danced across the plains until night came.

The people in the camp who were her special friends had been very worried, and early in the morning they came to look for her. Brolga saw them coming and hurried to meet them. They stopped and stared as this tall bird, quite strange to them, came near and began to dance. Entranced by its grace they watched, and as the feet stepped and leapt, and the wings waved and flapped, they were each reminded of their Brolga.

Suddenly they guessed what had happened. "Brolga," they called. "Brolga, can it really be you?" And Brolga nodded and danced even more exotically. Then they knew that it really was their Brolga.

They begged her to return to camp with them, and she came. The people continued to call her by her name, and they watched over her and protected her from further harm. Throughout her long life she charmed everyone with her gentle ways and dreamlike dancing.

Brolga birds still love to perform their beautiful dances. And the people who watch them still admire and protect them.

The Rainbow Bridge

[Promoting Self-esteem]

When your self-esteem is high, you are in control of your life. You feel powerful and you know how to make things happen. I wonder how often you feel like this. As we grow older and learn the ways of the world, self-doubt grows and we become defensive so that we can 'protect' ourselves. And as we lose the feeling of trust we were born with, so we lose our self-esteem in equal measure. Unless we can overcome such learning blocks, there can be little hope of success. Promoting self-esteem is all about helping people to reclaim their birthright. And the first step on the path to achieving this could be crossing the Rainbow Bridge.

The Rainbow Bridge

I started by crawling on my hands and knees before I progressed to taking a few faltering steps. However, I never strayed far afield and I always returned back home to the safety of my mother, whom I still felt part of.

Eventually, I grew in courage and became more ambitious but even so I always returned home to her again. I would spend my time walking under the canopy of the forest, following the path of dead leaves, the fallen dreams, until I came to the Rainbow Bridge that crossed over the River of Forgotten Origins. Even though I often went there to look over to the other side enveloped in mist, I still didn't feel ready to cross it.

And so it went on, day after day, month after month and year after year until, without my realising it, I had turned old and grey and my mother was no longer there for me to return to. I found myself cut off from all that surrounded me, lost and wandering in a foreign land.

What I needed was to reconnect with what I'd been part of, to rediscover the knowledge that I'd been born with, that everything lives and that all things are related so that if I hurt one of my relations then I hurt myself. And the only way to renew my link was to cross over the Rainbow Bridge, to the other side.

I took strength from my helper the panther. I climbed on to his back and felt his power under me as he took me back to my starting point. But from there I had to go it alone. So I closed my eyes tightly and started the crossing, to a place where I could never feel alone again and where I would be comforted by all my family – like the threads of the spider's web, all interconnected. All I had to do was cross over and the illusion of isolation would come to an end.

Now, every minute of every hour of every day, I try to hold on to my vision. For every time that my thread in the web snaps, I am disconnected from the life-force and vulnerable again.

A Guided Visualisation: The Rainbow Bridge

SCRIPT FOR THE GUIDE: (To be read in a gentle trance-inducing voice.) Make yourself comfortable and close your eyes. Take a few deep breaths to help you relax. Feel the tension disappear stage by stage from the top of your head to the tips of your toes. Let your surroundings fade away as you gradually sink backwards through time and actuality and pass through the gateway of reality into the dreamtime. (When the participants are fully relaxed, begin the next stage.)

You're standing on the bank of a river and the grass is wet from the early morning rain. Hear the sound of the water lapping against the shore and see a family of ducks gliding past. Everything you've always wanted lies on the other side of the river, enveloped in the early morning mist. What is it that you've always wanted but have never truly believed to be possible? What has always seemed to be too good to be true and just beyond your reach? You have a minute of clock time, equal to all the time you need to reflect on these innermost desires....

There's no bridge, the river's too wide and dangerous to swim across, and you're wondering what you can do. Just when it seems you have no choice but to give up, the solution presents itself – as it always does if you have faith. A rainbow materialises in the sky, bridging the gap between the two banks. Do you have the faith to cross over? Can you believe strongly enough in the dream to turn it into reality? Can you take control *of your life? The time is ripe and you know you'll never have a better chance. You step onto the rainbow and start to make your way across, looking only straight ahead towards the future. And as I start to count down slowly from ten, you gradually bridge the gap between the two banks. And with each step you take, the vision of what awaits you becomes clearer 10 – 9 – 8 – 7 – 6 – 5 – 4 – 3 – 2 – 1 – and the final step on to dry land. Take a minute of clock time, equal to all the time you need, to enjoy this vision of your future success....*

Before you return from the dreamtime, you are allowed to choose something to take back with you to keep your vision fresh in your mind, to help you focus on the fact that its attainment is in your hands. Take a minute of clock time, equal to all the time you need, to choose what you're going to bring back with you to prove that what you have had a taste of can be more than just a dream....

Now the time has come for you to return again. And as I count slowly up to ten, you make your way back across the bridge to the present time and place and back to the point you started from 1 – 2 – 3 – 4 – 5 – 6 – 7 – 8 – 9 – 10 – and home again.

Open your eyes now and stretch your arms and legs. Welcome back! Take a few minutes in silence to make some notes on the experiences you had on your journeys, which you can then share with the rest of the group/make a note of in your dream journal.

To And From the Great Mystery

I pray to be at one with the Great Mystery again
But the cell I've enclosed myself in
Cuts me off from the Life-Force
Wakan-Tanka
Help me to reach you again
And merge back into your wholeness

I feel you calling out to me
And with each passing day
Your voice grows inside me
To put aside my daily meanderings
To turn to you and find my life's mission

May Raven come to me in my dreams tonight
And transport me to my calling
So that I may find my rightful place
In the Great Mystery

The time is ripe now
For me to open my wings and fly with you
Outside the vision of my feeble eyes
Above the clouds that envelop me

Wakan-Tanka
Hear me calling
Help me and all my relations to reach you again
And merge back into your wholeness.

Note: For followers of Native American ways, Wakan-Tanka is the primal energy source of the Great Mystery. The Great Mystery lives in everything, is everything and encompasses everything in Creation.

The Road to Elfinland

[Successes and Failures –
Steps in the Learning Process]

The Road To Elfinland is described in the traditional ballad of Thomas the Rhymer and the account could well be based on a shamanic journey undertaken in pagan times. To enjoy the journey it's important to be able to see experiences along the way, both the positive and negative, as steps in the learning process. And as long as you learn from the experiences you have, there is no reason to regard anything untoward that happens along the way as a mistake. It's important to see both successes and failures as events in the unfolding of who we are. That's all very well in theory but not so easy to put into practice. Hopefully, the healing power of metaphor can help to reinforce the message.

Alice meets the Cheshire Cat

… The Cat only grinned when it saw Alice. It looked good-natured, she thought: still it had very long claws and a great many teeth, so she felt that it ought to be treated with respect.

" Cheshire Puss," she began, rather timidly, as she did not at all know whether it would like the name: however, it only grinned a little wider.

"It's pleased so far," thought Alice, and she went on.

"Would you tell me, please, which way I ought to go from here?"

"That depends a good deal on where you want to get to," said the Cat.

"I don't much care where —" said Alice.

"Then it doesn't matter which way you go," said the Cat.

"— so long as I get somewhere," Alice added as an explanation.

"Oh, you're sure to do that," said the Cat, "if you only walk long enough."

– Lewis Carroll, *Alice in Wonderland*

Far Journey Chant

We far journey
We far travel
Over new trails
Upon new paths

Keep us well
Guide us true
Over new trails
Upon new paths

Bring us back
See us home
Where loved ones wait
Our safe return.
— Mary Summer Rain, *Ancient Echoes*

A Guided Visualisation: The Road to Elfinland

SCRIPT FOR THE GUIDE: *(To be read in a gentle trance-inducing voice.) Make yourself comfortable and close your eyes. Take a few deep breaths to help you relax. Feel the tension disappear stage by stage from the top of your head to the tips of your toes. Let your surroundings fade away as you gradually sink backwards through time and actuality and pass through the gateway of reality into the dreamtime. (When the participants are fully relaxed, begin the next stage.)*

You're standing in the middle of a field of corn and there are three pathways in front of you – the Road to Heaven, the Road to Hell and the Road to Elfinland. The Road to Elfinland is the one you take, to meet with the little people.

The further you walk along the road into the forest, the lighter you feel. All the worldly cares you were carrying around with you fade away and you feel refreshed, renewed and ready for adventure. You have a minute of clock time, equal to all the time you need, to enjoy your new-found sense of weightlessness and to appreciate the enchanting landscape that surrounds you....

In the undergrowth you hear the tinkle of a bell but when you get to the place the sound was coming from, you find nothing there. You then hear the sound of the bell coming from the opposite direction. Once again you follow the tinkle but once again there's nothing to be found. It seems as if someone's playing a game with you. Feeling frustrated at your lack of success in finding the source of the sound, you sit down on a tree stump to take a breather. Just then someone taps you on the shoulder and makes you jump. You turn round to find a fairy facing you, who comes up no higher than your knee.

"Welcome to Elfinland. My name is Tinkerbell and I have the power to take you on a magical journey, wherever you'd like to go." You have a minute of clock time, equal to all the time you need, to let Tinkerbell transport you to your chosen destination....

"I'm afraid the time has come for me to take you back to the forest where you found me – all good things must come to an end. But to remind you of this journey, the holiday of a lifetime, you can take back a souvenir with you." You have a minute of clock time, equal to all the time you need, to choose your souvenir....

Tinkerbell waves her magic wand and in a flash you find yourself transported back to the tree stump, with your fairy friend sitting on your lap. You thank her for the opportunity she gave you and say goodbye for it's time to make your way home. You return the same way you came, back along the pathway to the cornfield, back to the place you started from. Welcome home!

Open your eyes now and stretch your arms and legs. Take a few minutes in silence to make some notes on the experiences you had on your journeys, which you can then share with the rest of the group/make a note of in your dream journal.

To conclude this section, a story from China about two men, one good and one bad, some extra special birds and a beautiful princess. Before you read or listen to it, you might like to write your own version of the story, then compare it with the original!

The Two Travellers

Once upon a time there were two men, one good and one bad, who went on a journey together. The good man shared his food with his companion until it was all finished.

The good man then asked: "Can I have some of your food now?"

"Certainly not," said the other and he got very angry. He blinded his unfortunate partner, stole everything he had, and left him alone in the middle of a forest.

The good man heard some birds singing in a tree and decided to climb it to be safe from any wild animals until morning when he could think of a way to continue his journey.

He discovered he could understand the language of the birds. As he listened, he learnt from them that if he washed his eyes in the dew of that place he would be able to see again. He also learnt from them that the king's daughter was dying but that a special flower that grew next to the tree could save her.

He immediately washed his eyes in the dew and found he could see again. Then he went to the Palace with the special flower and saved the Princess. The Princess fell in love with the good man who saved her life and they got married.

They lived happily together until the bad man returned to discover the secret of his companion's success.

The good man told him about the birds in the tree and he went there to hear them for himself. He found he could understand their conversation and this is what they said. "Here's the bad man who blinded the husband of the Princess and stole all his money." Then they flew down from the tree and ate him for breakfast.

If the good man in the tale had not been blinded, he never would have discovered how to save the dying princess. The story has been included to provide an illustration of how we can profit from the negative as well as the positive experiences we have. And you and/or your clients might now like to reflect on what you have learnt from the adversity you have had to face in your own lives.

The Book
of Life
[Taking Control of your Life]

We can regard ourselves as victims of circumstance, or learn how to take control of our lives – the choice is ours. The Book of Life presents us with an opportunity to clarify our dreams and then to follow up the process by dancing them awake. And a journey to meet Otchopintre, a spirit from Georgian folklore who appears in the spring to breathe new life into nature, provides the energy and resolve for the process.

A Guided Visualisation: The Book of Life

SCRIPT FOR THE GUIDE: (To be read in a gentle trance-inducing voice.) Make yourself comfortable and close your eyes. Take a few deep breaths to help you relax. Feel the tension disappear stage by stage from the top of your head to the tips of your toes. Let your surroundings fade away as you gradually sink backwards through time and actuality and pass through the gateway of reality into the dreamtime. (When the participants are fully relaxed, begin the next stage.)

Today's a very special day for you because you're being given an opportunity to look into your future, an opportunity most people will never have so make sure you don't waste it.

You're standing at the foot of a mountain with a winding path ahead of you leading up to the top. The weather's hot and sticky and the climb is steep but you're determined and refuse to be deterred. Eventually you reach the summit where you find a palace cut out of crystal glittering in the sunlight. You have a minute of clock time, equal to all the time you need, to take a breather and to appreciate the building now facing you....

Now the moment has come to enter the palace and you walk through the arched doorway into the interior. Once inside you follow a labyrinth of corridors until you eventually reach the heart of the palace underneath the main spire. You climb up three steps to an altar stone where you find a large open book, a quill and a bottle of ink. On the top of the left-hand page you find your name written in gold and a forecast for the next five years of your life. You have a minute of clock time, equal to all the time you need, to study what it says....

Why has the quill been left on the altar together with the bottle of ink? Because you have the right to add a sentence of your own to the forecast, something you long for and hope will come true. You have a minute of clock time, equal to all the time you need, to add your dream to the page....

Remember you have the power to dance this dream awake and all you need is faith. And now the time has come for you to return, back through the labyrinth of corridors and down the steep path, back to the place you started from. Welcome home!

Open your eyes now and stretch your arms and legs. Welcome back! Take a few minutes in silence to make some notes on the experiences you had on your journeys, which you can then share with the rest of the group/make a note of in your dream journal.

The Book of Life

On the top of sacred mountain
From the rock foundations rises crystal palace
And in the womb-like chamber that lies within its centre
On a crystal dais I found the Book of Life

I turned the pages to find they stopped at the present
For it was up to me to fill in what comes next
Then to set out with my new-found sense of purpose
And to dance those pages awake

Whenever I lose my way, I'll see those pages before me
To guide me back on to my path
And each time I'm blessed with a new dream
I'll return there to add it to my list.

A Guided Visualisation: The Magic Touch of Otchopintre

SCRIPT FOR THE GUIDE: (To be read in a gentle trance-inducing voice.) Make yourself comfortable and close your eyes. Take a few deep breaths to help you relax. Breathe in the white light and breathe out all your tightness. Feel the tension disappear stage by stage from the top of your head to the tips of your toes. Let your surroundings fade away as you gradually sink backwards through time and actuality and pass through the gateway of reality into the dreamtime. (When the participants are fully relaxed, begin the next stage.)

You're walking along a path through a beautiful forest. Feel your feet on the ground and see the sunlight filtering through the gaps in the canopy of trees overhead. Hear the birdsong and the crackling of twigs underfoot and smell the rich, damp forest air. You follow the path as it winds its way through the forest until you come to a clearing.

You see something moving in the distance – it looks like the branches of a tree with legs walking towards you. And as it comes closer, the picture gets clearer and you see who it is. Who can it be? There's only one answer. It must be Otchopintre, followed by a procession of animals basking in the sunlight that trails behind him. And you have a minute of clock time, equal to all the time you need, to study the figure now standing before you and to enjoy this special moment....

It's been a difficult year for you and you're tired after all the efforts you've made and the hardships you've had to face. But Otchopintre points his magical fingers towards you and you feel the new life start to surge through your veins. And you have a minute of clock time, equal to all the time you need, to appreciate Otchopintre's healing touch as he revitalises you and fills you with energy....

And now that you feel refreshed and ready for the year that lies ahead of you, give thanks to Otchopintre and promise that you'll put your new-found energy to good use. And you have a minute of clock time, equal to all the time you need, to describe your future plans and to assure him of your commitment....

Now the time has come for your journey home. But as you make your way back along the path, your body feels a lot lighter this time, as if you've shed a heavy weight from your shoulders, and you're feeling full of enthusiasm for the tasks that lie ahead of you – secure in the knowledge you have the determination and energy to accomplish them. And you follow the pathway, back through the forest, back, back, through time and space, back to the place you started from.

Take a deep breath and let it out, open your eyes and smile at the first person you see. Stretch your arms and legs, then stamp your feet on the ground to make sure you're really home. Take a few minutes in silence to make some notes on the experiences you had on your journeys, which you can then share with the rest of the group/make a note of in your dream journal.

The Forest Guardian

The charred remains of tree stumps are my scars
Time to plant flowers to call the butterflies there
Time for new life to grow from the remnants of the past

Howling at the moon will serve no purpose
Rise above such petty issues
And let nothing deter you from your path

Be fluid like the water and adaptable
So obstacles provide you with opportunities
To grow into something new.

The
Healing Waters
[Learning how to Value what We already Have]

We have an unfortunate tendency to take natural resources for granted but without them where would we be? Take water as an example. The human body is made up of a minimum 60% of water and without water there could be no life. Tribal peoples have always been aware of their dependency on such resources and their traditional tales reflect this. *The Healing Waters* is a Native American tale about the healing power of water, *The Healing Waters of Ratcha* can be found in the Caucasus, and *The Lady of the Lake* comes from Arthurian legend.

We have allowed ourselves to become brainwashed into wanting what we can't afford to buy (and what we don't really need) instead of learning how to value what we already have. The tales and journeys that follow help us to rediscover what so-called 'primitive' tribal peoples have always known – how to tap into these resources.

The Healing Waters

The snows of winter lay as heavily on the ground as did the sorrow in the hearts of the people. Plague had struck the camp leaving many people dying and dead. Having lost his parents, brothers, sisters and children, Nekumonta now faced the death of his beloved wife, Shanewis. In despair he said to himself, "I must do something to help her or she will not see the light of one more morning. I will go and find the healing herbs planted by the Great Manitou."

Nekumonta made Shanewis as comfortable as he could, placing food and water near her. Then he covered her with a soft fur robe and said, "I must go to find some herbs to cure you. I will return very soon. Please, wait for me." Embracing her gently, he said goodbye and set off on his journey.

Wherever he went he saw only ice and snow. For three days and three nights he travelled along the frozen ground asking any animal who came in sight where the herbs might be but none answered. On the third night, weak from lack of food, Nekumonta caught his foot on an upturned branch and dropped into the snow. Too tired to free himself, he soon fell asleep right where he was. The animals of the forest came and saw him sleeping. They looked at his kind face and saw his loving heart. They prayed to the Great Manitou to help him find the healing herbs for his beloved Shanewis.

The Great Manitou heard the plea of the animals and sent a messenger to appear in the dreams of Nekumonta. In the dream he saw his beautiful Shanewis alive and smiling, singing a song which sounded like the music of a waterfall. Then, suddenly, he saw a waterfall and heard a voice calling, "Look for us, Nekumonta. When you find us Shanewis will live. We are the Healing Waters of the Great Manitou."

When Nekumonta awoke he searched all over for the Healing Waters but could not find them. Then he decided to look beneath the frozen ground. He was so weak he could barely dig; only his spirit kept him going but he continued and at last the hidden waters came into view. The Healing Waters streamed out carrying life and well-being wherever they went.

Nekumonta bathed in the waters and once more felt well and strong. He made a jar of clay and baked it in the fire until he knew it would hold the waters while he returned to Shanewis. He sped homeward as fast as he could go. His sorrow changed to joy as he thought of seeing Shanewis once more, alive and well.

When he arrived in the village and saw the sorrowing villagers he told them all about the Healing Waters and urged them to go and bring some water back. He found Shanewis very close to death and hoped he had not arrived too late.

Nekumonta brushed some of the Healing Waters on her parched lips and poured tiny drops of water down her throat. She fell into a gentle sleep. When she awoke, her fever was gone.

Nekumonta's heart was filled with great happiness. He and Shanewis lived together for many years. The Healing Waters helped to rid the village of the plague. Nekumonta was given the name of "Chief of the Healing Waters" so that everyone would know who had given them the gift from the Great Manitou.

– *Storytelling in Education and Therapy,*
  Jessica Kingsley Publishers Ltd

Exercise for Teachers of English as a Foreign Language

Pre-listening: *We have an unfortunate tendency to take natural resources for granted but without them where would we be? Take water as an example. The human body is made up of a minimum 60% of water and without water there could be no life. Invite the students to brainstorm all the uses of water in groups.* A representative from each group can then board the lists for the whole class to see.

Tribal peoples have always been aware of their dependency on such resources and their traditional tales reflect this. Today's story is a Native American tale about the healing power of water.

Post-listening: Match the idioms on the left with the explanations on the right. There are more explanations than you need so make sure you select the correct ones!

1. You must have felt like a fish out of water.
2. You seem to be finding it difficult to keep your head above water.
3. You've gone through fire and water, haven't you?
4. You're spending money like water.
5. What you said doesn't hold water.
6. You can lead a horse to water but you can't make him drink.
7. You seem to have taken to your new job like a duck to water.
8. You always pour cold water on my hopes.
9. Your remarks were like water off a duck's back.

a. I can see that you've settled down really well.
b. I've cried a lot since then.
c. I imagine you felt rather ill-at-ease.
d. It's been a real struggle for you, hasn't it?
e. It seems to be hard for you stay out of debt.
f. I wish you wouldn't be so discouraging.
g. There have been a lot of changes.
h. There's no point in forcing people to do things against their will.
i. What you said had no effect on me.

10. A lot of water has flowed under the bridge since then.

j. What you said was very hurtful.

k. You help me to keep my feet on the ground.

l. Your argument is not convincing.

m. You're not a very good swimmer, are you?

n. You're rather careful with money, aren't you?

o. You're rather extravagant.

Answers: 1 – c, 2 – e, 3 – d, 4 – o, 5 – l, 6 – h, 7 – a, 8 – f, 9 – i, 10 – g

Ask everyone in the class to select a number from one to twenty. Invite the students to write about an important experience Nekumonta had at the age this number represents. Explain that the memory of this experience is what kept Nekumonta going during his difficult journey.

A Guided Visualisation: The Healing Waters of Ratcha

SCRIPT FOR THE GUIDE: *(To be read in a gentle trance-inducing voice.) Make yourself comfortable and close your eyes. Take a few deep breaths to help you relax. Breathe in the white light and breathe out all your tightness. Feel the tension disappear stage by stage from the top of your head to the tips of your toes. Let your surroundings fade away as you gradually sink backwards through time and actuality and pass through the gateway of reality into the dreamtime. (When the participants are fully relaxed, begin the next stage.)*

You're climbing up the side of a mountain in the Caucasus and you're up to your knees in snow. An icy cold wind is blowing against you but you're determined to reach the ledge above and nothing is going to stop you. Higher and higher you climb and you're all on your own, having left the world you're familiar with far behind you. And everywhere you look, there's nothing but snow – stretching as far as the eyes can see. Each step you take gets more difficult but you know you've nearly reached your destination, where you'll be able to find what you've come in search of. Just one more step and you're on the ledge, the mouth of the cave straight ahead. You have a minute of clock time now, equal to all the time you need, to recover from the climb and to admire the breathtaking view all around you....

And now the time has come for you to enter. The cave is almost transparent, as if made of crystal, and you walk down the tunnel towards the light. Music fills the air like the sound of wind chimes and the tunnel opens out into a dome-shaped cavern where you're almost blinded by the brilliant light. You have a minute of clock time, equal to all the time you need, to gradually get used to the light and to appreciate the beauty that lies in the heart of the mountain....

In the centre of the cavern there's a rock pool filled with icy cold water and you walk towards it. You cup your hands together and scoop out some water to drink. Never before have you tasted such goodness. It seems to fill your body with liquid crystal, refreshing and revitalising you. You have a minute of clock time, equal to all the time you need, to appreciate the sensation, and to feel your body filling with vitality....

Now that you've drunk your fill, it's time to return. But you know now that whenever life becomes too much to bear and you feel that you can't go on, you can come back again to Ratcha to recharge your batteries, and that the healing waters will always be there for you. You turn your back on the cavern and return to the ledge, ready to make your descent. And as you lower yourself down the side of the mountain by rope, you know that you've left all your problems behind you and that you're returning filled with new-found energy, eager for the future that awaits you. Join me as I count down slowly from ten, to return to the place you started from. 10 – 9 – 8 – 7 – 6 – 5 – 4 – 3 – 2 – 1 – and welcome home!

Take a deep breath and let it out, open your eyes and smile at the first person you see. Stretch your arms and legs, then stamp your feet on the ground to make sure you're really back. Take a few minutes in silence to make some notes on the experiences you had on your journeys, which you can then share with the rest of the group/make a note of in your dream journal.

From earliest times, all over the world, water has been associated with spirits and gods. When Christianity came to England, the priests did not allow the people to look upon a well or spring as the home of a pagan god but, with the cleverness which is typical of the early Christians, they kept the well or spring as a holy place by dedicating it to the Virgin Mary or to a Saint.

The custom of decorating wells still exists in the county of Derbyshire, and of these the best-known takes place in the village of Tissington. One story goes that the people of the village dressed the well for the first time in 1615, after a very long period without rain, between March and September. During this time the Tissington wells were the only ones to provide water, not only for the people and animals of the village, but for those of all the other nearby villages and farms as well. Another story goes right back to 1350, after the Black Death had visited that part of England in the years 1348–49. It seems that the only village where not one person or animal died of the Black Death was Tissington, because the water from the wells was so pure.

Until the beginning of the eighteenth century, the wells were simply decorated with flowers, but by 1818 the decorations had become more complex. The villagers make a large wooden frame and fill it with soft mud. They then fill the frame with a picture, using flowers, small stones, leaves, and other natural materials. Nothing man-made is allowed to be used. On Ascension Day, the fortieth day after Easter Sunday, the completed picture is taken in its frame to the well, and placed behind it. Some Derbyshire families have been well-dressers for generations, learning this beautiful and unique rural craft from father to son.

The Lady of the Lake

The Lady of the Lake may be the literary form of a Celtic water deity. According to legend, she is the one who gives Arthur's sword, Excalibur, to him and the one who receives it back when it is thrown by Sir Bedivere, after Arthur receives his mortal wound. She is called Viviane or Eviene or Niviene or Nina or Nimue and so may be several different women, all referred to by the title Lady of the Lake. In some romances, she is said to have been responsible for raising Lancelot, in others for being the enchantress who captivated Merlin (some texts say that she also killed him), and in another, that she was Merlin's scribe, who recorded his prophecies.

A Guided Visualisation: A Meeting with Viviane, The Lady of the Lake

SCRIPT FOR THE GUIDE: (To be read in a gentle trance-inducing voice.) Make yourself comfortable and close your eyes. Take a few deep breaths to help you relax. Feel the tension disappear stage by stage from the top of your head to the tips of your toes. Let your surroundings fade away as you gradually sink backwards through time and actuality and pass through the gateway of reality into the dreamtime. (When the participants are fully relaxed, begin the next stage.)

Step into the forest and find yourself enveloped in a thick swirling fog. Gradually it clears and you find yourself standing at the edge of a lake. Feel the warmth of the sun beating down on you and smell the scent of the wild flowers that grow along the bank. Now lean across and look into the water. Notice the fish darting to and fro underneath the surface. Scoop up and drink a handful of the cool sweet-tasting water, and feel relaxed and content. You have a minute of clock time, equal to all the time you need, to appreciate the scene....

Just then, from nowhere, the most beautiful and enchanting woman appears and gently approaches you. It's impossible to take your eyes from her face. She glows with a radiance that is not of this world. Trembling with emotion, you're about to speak but she anticipates your thoughts before you have the chance to voice them.

"Men know me as the Lady of the Lake but my other names are Truth, Compassion, Justice and Hope. Ask me your questions and I will reply with honesty, integrity and enlightenment." You have a minute of clock time, equal to all the time you need, to listen to her words of wisdom....

"Although you will see me no more, I will always be at the side of those who seek to journey within. Rest assured your journey through this life will end with light."

The swirling fog then descends and envelops you again and the scene that lay before you fades into the distance.

Now the time has come to make your way back to the place where you started from and to take all the beautiful things you've experienced with you, everything you've seen, heard, felt, smelled or tasted. And remember that whenever you want you can return to this place again to enjoy the special effect it has on you.

Take a deep breath, release it, open your eyes and stretch your arms and legs. Stamp your feet on the ground to make sure you're really back. Welcome home! Take a few minutes in silence to make some notes on the experiences you had on your journeys, which you can then share with the rest of the group/make a note of in your dream journal.

"She dwells down in a deep calm —
 whatsoever storms may shake the world
 — and when the surface rolls
 has the power to walk the waters like our Lord."
— Alfred Lord Tennyson, *The Coming of Arthur*

The
Standing People
[Reconnecting with the Life-force]

In a number of traditions the Tree is used to access other realities – to reach the Upper World by climbing its trunk and the Lower World by travelling down through its roots. Poles can even be found through the centre of dwellings used by shamans and accounts of these practices can be found in Eliade's book. He wrote that the tree expresses the sacrality of the world, its fertility and perenniality. It is related to the ideas of creation, fecundity, and initiation, and finally to the idea of absolute reality and immortality, representing the universe in continual regeneration. There is the tree that Eve ate the apple from in the Garden of Eden and the symbol of The Tree of Life used in Kabalistic practice. In England there is the tradition of dancing round the Maypole and there is the Native American Sundance Ceremony which also takes place round a pole. Idiomatic language reflects the importance of trees to us too – family trees, for example.

Native Americans refer to the Standing People and the Stone People. They teach that the Standing People and all others of the Plant Kingdom are the givers who constantly provide for the needs of others and the Stone People hold energy for the Earth Mother and records of all that has happened in a specific place.

The rain forests are the perfect example of how trees provide for our needs. Furniture, chewing gum, rayon, fabric, books, paper, pencils, kitchen matches, spices and seasonings, fruit, nuts, rope, tyres, and herbal remedies are just a few of the gifts from the Standing People. Most significantly of all, they provide us with the oxygen upon which we depend to survive. They can teach us the importance of establishing roots deep into the Earth to receive spiritual nurturing as well as the reconnective energy that keeps our bodies healthy. Without these roots, we lose our Earth-Connection and can no longer walk in balance. We all know, for example, how therapeutic a walk in the country can be to alleviate stress.

It is emotions, not logic, that drive our attention, meaning-making and memory. This suggests the importance of trainers eliciting curiosity, suspense, excitement, joy, laughter and even sadness. Moreover, as a result of recently acquired knowledge of how the brain works, we now know that an experience with a powerful attachment to emotions or feelings is more likely to be retained in the long-term memory. That is why the use of ceremony to follow the stories and visualisations presented in this book can reinforce the impact of the material, especially when it is devised by the participants themselves – Fire Ceremonies to burn what no longer serves us and to leave the past behind; Water Ceremonies for purification; and hugging trees to help us reconnect with the Life-Force. Trees can also provide answers to the questions that trouble us. Stand facing the four directions against a tree of your choice, repeat the question that is on your mind at each location and listen to the answers that come to you. If you feel comfortable making use of ceremony, so will the people you work with because you will then be able to facilitate the process with conviction. The word enthusiasm (en theos) means 'the God within' and is the spark that lights the candle.

Tree Poem 1

A curse on trees –
Fixed in the ground
Forced to take note
Of their surroundings
And to be patient
With whatever they may have as company
Be it the sun beating down on their backs
Or the pounding rain
From which there is no escape

A blessing in disguise on trees —
Fixed in the ground
Taught the lesson of tolerance
And bound to face up to reality
In all its baffling guises
To discover what, in our impatience
We never have time for

Wise ones
May we acknowledge and study under you
What comes naturally?

Tree Poem 2
How still are these trees
their countenances free from
the day's turbulence
I watch the shaded planes of their
faces placid in the evening
As their breath films the air

Oh, they are wise these trees
their roots seeking the earth's deep
crystal arteries
to nurture and draw up to the sky

How regal this one face
set towards me
the stirring leaves animating
its expression
accentuating the green cheekbones
this patient face framed
by its head-dress of summer foliage
and dissolving into the shadowed fabric
of the night

How still are these green chieftains
of our land.

Note: The two poems were taken from a magazine called *Medicine Ways*, Issue 4 published by Alawn Tickhill in 1989. For further details, the publisher can be contacted at 35 Wilson Avenue, Deal, Kent CT14 9NL.

A Guided Visualisation: The Standing People

SCRIPT FOR THE GUIDE: (To be read in a gentle trance-inducing voice.) Make yourself comfortable and close your eyes. Take a few deep breaths to help you relax. Feel the tension disappear stage by stage from the top of your head to the tips of your toes. Let your surroundings fade away as you gradually sink backwards through time and actuality and pass through the gateway of reality into the dreamtime.

The forest in all civilisations is a mysterious place, the source of tales and legends involving men, women, children, animals and fairies. However, we should also not forget the Standing People (trees) and the Stone People, witnesses to history and sources of power and knowledge. Universal rites and customs have been profoundly marked by the influence of the forest, passed down from generation to generation by the oral traditions of so-called primitive societies. Today you have the opportunity to journey into the heart of one of these enchanted places and to tap into the wisdom stored within its depths.

Your physical eyes are closed but your third eye is wide open. Let it guide you on a path into the heart of the forest and open your senses to the sights, sounds and smells you witness on your way – the leaves that form a canopy over your head, the sounds of the creatures that make the forest their home, and the scents produced by the greenery that surrounds you.

You have a minute of clock time, equal to all the time you need, to appreciate the scene you are part of....

You notice a tree that stands out from all the rest, a tree that seems to draw you to it, a tree that seems to be calling to you. Put your arms around its trunk and listen to what it has to tell you. Perhaps you have a specific question you would like the tree to answer or you simply want to tap into its power and wisdom. You have a minute of clock time, equal to all the time you need, to commune with the Standing Person....

You continue on your way and this time a Stone Person calls to you. Pick the stone up with respect and hold it in your cupped palms. Examine its different facets. What pictures do they conjure up for you? You have a minute of clock time, equal to all the time you need, to learn from your new companion....

Place the Stone Person back where you found it and give thanks for the lessons you learnt. The time has now come for you to make your way home, back along the path that led you to this place and back to the place you started from. Welcome home!

Open your eyes now and stretch your arms and legs. Take a few minutes in silence to make some notes on the experiences you had on your journeys, which you can then share with the rest of the group/make a note of in your dream journal.

Moontime & Sacred Space
[A Time for Looking Within]

Why isn't it light 24 hours a day? Why do we have night and why is the sun brighter than the moon? The Creation Myths that follow answer these questions and they come from the Philippines.

Why there is Night

Once upon a time the Sun and the Moon were both very bright and it was always daytime.

The Sun had no wife so the Moon laughed at him. "Why are you always laughing at me?" the Sun complained. "I'm getting very tired of you."

The Moon answered, "I'm laughing at you because you have no wife and you must cook your food yourself. A God who cooks his own food! Ha! Ha! Ha!"

"Stop laughing at me at once!" the Sun ordered. "The problem with you is that you have no respect." But the Moon didn't stop laughing and the Sun got very angry. He picked up a handful of coals from his fire and he threw them into the Moon's face.

So now the Moon can't shine so brightly and he hides for half the day because he's ashamed of his appearance. And that's how we have day and night.

Why the Moon is not as bright as the Sun

A long time ago the Moon was brighter than the Sun. The people worked when the Moon was out and slept when the Sun came out. The Sun was often jealous of the Moon because it was much brighter than himself.

One day, the Sun put a heavy boulder on the limbs of a pine tree. Then he told the Moon, as they passed through the forest, "I was told that there is much gold under that stone. If you take away the stone, you can have the gold." Eagerly, the Moon did as he was told. The stone was heavy, and it took some time to lift. As soon as the Moon had moved the boulder away, the tree's branches sprang up and scratched him badly on the face. Since then, he has not shone as brightly as the Sun, so that now the Sun is brighter than the Moon. The two have always been enemies since then.

The tales above could be used as a springboard into a creative writing and/or story telling session. Arrange the participants in groups to make up stories for one of the following titles: How The Sun Came To Be/How The Rivers Came To Be/How The Stars Came To Be/How The Mountains Came To Be, etc. They can then share their stories or even act them out.

The Moon has traditionally set the time for important undertakings, for the start of new cycles or for making resolutions. For Native Americans, the Moon Lodge was the place where women gathered during their menstrual time to be at one with each other and the changes taking place in their bodies. It was a time of retreat. Setting aside an extended period of time for contemplation is a feature of many different faiths, from Catholic to Buddhist, and can provide the opportunity to look within and to recharge your batteries. Church father St Augustine confirmed the validity of introspection, believing that scrutiny of inner experiences provides a vehicle for personal communion with God. And Hermann Hesse said that loneliness is the way by which destiny endeavours to lead man to himself. Although in one sense a retreat can be considered to be a time of inactivity, without such downtime for internal processing the future can't take hold of the present so it can also be seen as an essential part of life. You know only too well how irritable people can become when deprived of this time for themselves. So however busy we may find ourselves, we ignore the need for such times at our peril.

The Shining

And so I turn to the full moon
Naked as the day I was born
Shine down on the crystal ball
That lies embedded within me
So I encompass the shining
The mystery that I'm part of

And now I'm running with Panther
We go to the watering hole
Where we drink with all our fellows
And where we share the same water
On which our bodies depend
Water of love which unites us

We are the power and the shining
We are one and there's no other
When we fight we fight with ourselves
That's why it hurts us so deeply
And that's how the world is scarred
When we forget our common course

And so I turn to the full moon
Naked as the day I was born
To shine down and so awaken
The love that lies within us all
The power of love that unites us
The power that holds us together.

A Guided Visualisation: The Full Moon

SCRIPT FOR THE GUIDE: (To be read in a gentle trance-inducing voice.) Make yourself comfortable and close your eyes. Take a few deep breaths to help you relax. Feel the tension disappear stage by stage from the top of your head to the tips of your toes. Let your surroundings fade away as you gradually sink backwards through time and actuality and pass through the gateway of reality into the dreamtime. (When the participants are fully relaxed, begin the next stage.)

It's night time and the middle of winter. You're standing on the side of a hill, exposed to the elements, the full force of the ice-cold wind blowing against you, making your eyes water and your ears go numb. You can see nothing apart from the twinkling stars overhead and you feel totally alone. You have a minute of clock time, equal to all the time you need, to contemplate the great mystery that surrounds you....

Suddenly the full moon comes into view, rising from behind the hill in all its glory and bathing you in sacred light. The moonbeams shower down on you, connecting you with all that is, all that has been and all that will be. You have a minute of clock time, equal to all the time you need, to appreciate your connectedness and to consider the personal part you have to play in this equation....

The moonbeams penetrate right through to the depths of your being, recharging your batteries and filling you with power. You understand how you can be whoever you want to be and that all you need is faith. You have a minute of clock time, equal to all the time you need, to experience this sense of power.

Now the time has come to return from the dreamtime to ordinary reality, back to the place you started from. And as you make your way back down the side of the hill, try to hold on to everything you've experienced on your journey and remember you can return to the dreamtime again whenever you feel the need.

Open your eyes now and stretch your arms and legs. Welcome home! Take a few minutes in silence to make some notes on the experiences you had on your journeys, which you can then share with the rest of the group/make a note of in your dream journal.

Everything You Always Wanted to Know About the Moon

1. The light of the full moon is equivalent to that of a 15-watt lightbulb.

2. The moon is, on average, 239,000 miles away. The distance varies by 11 per cent as it follows an elliptical path around the Earth.

3. The moon is at least 4.6 billion years old and the rocks of its Highlands are older than any rocks on earth.

4. There is a superstition that when you see a new moon, you should turn the money over in your pocket for luck. It is also said that during a full moon, people tend to bleed more and that alcohol has a more potent effect.

5. For centuries the moon was associated with witchcraft, bad luck and the insane – the word 'lunatic' comes from the Latin for moon, luna. In Britain, the Lunacy Act of 1824 actually stated unequivocally that people went mad when the moon was full.

6. The recent discovery of ice on the moon could make it, according to NASA scientists, the most valuable piece of real estate in the solar system.

7. Our moon, the biggest in the solar system (roughly the same size across as Australia), has a gravity on its surface which is about one-sixth of that on Earth. And, although its gravitational force is minuscule by the time it reaches us, it still has an amazingly powerful effect on our planet. It certainly causes the tides – the moon's gravitational pull shifts a hundred billion tons of water out of the Bay of Fundy in Canada twice a day.

8. Oysters open, close and breed according to the tides. Normally, one would assume they were responding to the movement in the water around them, but experiments conducted by American Professor Brown in the 1960s seemed to prove otherwise. Oysters in light-proof containers of sea water experienced no tides, yet adjusted their movements to the upper and lower transits of the moon. For some reason, marine life seems able to 'tune in' to the moon without even seeing its light.

9. One of the oldest beliefs in folklore is that a full moon can turn a sane person into a madman. Robert Louis Stevenson's *Dr Jekyll and Mr Hyde* was inspired by the real life activities of Charles Hyde, who committed his horrendous activities during the full moon. In 1992 Christopher Gore began a sentence at Broadmoor hospital after being convicted of killing his parents. He is also suspected of murdering two others – all four linked to nights of the full moon.

10. As the lunar cycle and the solar year are often out of synch, around once every three years a month contains two full moons. The second full moon is called a 'blue moon' and because it is a rare event gives rise to the expression 'once in a blue moon'.

Exercises for Teachers of English as Foreign Language
Split the class into two groups. Hand out copies of Version A to the first group and copies of Version B to the second group. Then pair up the A with the B students and ask them to question each other to find the missing information:

Information Gap Activity: Version A

1. The light of the full moon is equivalent to ....
....

2. The moon is, on average, 239,000 miles away. (The distance varies by 11 per cent as it follows an elliptical path around the Earth.)

3. The moon is at least .... years old and the rocks of its Highlands are older than any rocks on earth.

4. There is a superstition that when you see a new moon, you should turn the money over in your pocket for luck. It is also said that during a full moon, people tend to .... and that drinking alcohol has a more potent effect.

5. For centuries the moon was associated with witchcraft, bad luck and the insane – the word 'lunatic' comes from the Latin for moon, luna. In Britain, the Lunacy Act of 1824 actually stated unequivocally that ....

6. The recent discovery of ice on the moon could make it, according to NASA scientists, the most valuable piece of real estate in the solar system.

7. Our moon, the biggest in the solar system (roughly the same size across as Australia), has a gravity on its surface which is about one-sixth of that on Earth. And, although its gravitational force is minuscule by the time it reaches us, it still has an amazingly powerful effect on our planet. It certainly causes the tides – the moon's gravitational pull shifts a hundred billion tons of water out of the Bay of Fundy in Canada twice a day.

8. Oysters open, close and breed according to the tides. Normally, one would assume they were responding to the movement in the water around them, but experiments conducted by ....
....seemed to prove otherwise. Oysters in light-proof containers of sea water experienced no tides, yet adjusted their movements to the upper and lower transits of the moon. For some reason, marine life seems able to 'tune in' to the moon without even seeing its light.

9. One of the oldest beliefs in folklore is..............................
Robert Louis Stevenson's *Dr Jekyll and Mr Hyde* was inspired by
the real life activities of Charles Hyde, who committed his horrendous activities during the full moon. In 1992 Christopher Gore
began a sentence at Broadmoor hospital after being convicted of
.... He is also suspected of murdering two others –
all four linked to nights of the full moon.

10. As the lunar cycle and the solar year are often out of synch,
around once every three years a month contains two full moons.
The second full moon is called a 'blue moon' and because it is a
rare event gives rise to the expression "once in a blue moon".

Information Gap Activity: Version B

1. The light of the full moon is equivalent to that of a 15-watt lightbulb.

2. The moon is, on average, ... miles away. (The distance
varies by 11 per cent as it follows an elliptical path around the
Earth.)

3. The moon is at least 4.6 billion years old and the rocks of its
Highlands are older than any rocks on earth.

4. There is a superstition that when you see a new moon, you
should .... It is also said
that during a full moon, people tend to bleed more and that
drinking alcohol has a more potent effect.

5. For centuries the moon was associated with witchcraft, bad
luck and the insane – the word 'lunatic' comes from ....
.... In Britain, the Lunacy Act of 1824 actually
stated unequivocally that people went mad when the moon was
full.

6. The recent discovery of ice on the moon could make it,
according to NASA scientists, ...
....

7. Our moon, the biggest in the solar system (roughly the same
size across as Australia), has a gravity on its surface which is about

one-sixth of that on Earth. And, although its gravitational force is minuscule by the time it reaches us, it still has an amazingly powerful effect on our planet. It certainly causes the tides – the moon's gravitational pull shifts a hundred billion tons of water out of the Bay of Fundy in Canada twice a day.

8. Oysters open, close and breed according to the tides. Normally, one would assume they were responding to the movement in the water around them, but experiments conducted by American Professor Brown in the 1960s seemed to prove otherwise. Oysters in light-proof containers of sea water experienced no tides, yet adjusted their movements to the upper and lower transits of the moon. For some reason, marine life seems able to ....
....

9. One of the oldest beliefs in folklore is that a full moon can turn a sane person into a madman. Robert Louis Stevenson's *Dr Jekyll and Mr Hyde* was inspired by ....
.... In 1992 Christopher Gore began a sentence at Broadmoor hospital after being convicted of killing his parents. He is also suspected of murdering two others – all four linked to nights of the full moon.

10. As the lunar cycle and the solar year are often out of synch, around once every three years ....
The second full moon is called a 'blue moon' and because it is a rare event gives rise to the expression "once in a blue moon".

The Inner and the Outer Circles

The inner circle, my sacred space
Where nobody is allowed to enter
The outer circle, to open to love
Where I can stretch out my roots and branches
The problem lies in the definitions
Which is which, where do the boundaries lie
How to distinguish one from the other
Where does the day end and the night begin
And there can be no mathematical formula
For it's something we can only feel
And what we need to be able to do
Is to place trust in our spirit helpers

Though we lie to ourselves, they never do
Because they are our only true teachers.

While some commuters can continue working on their laptops on their way to the office, others find the journey too distracting. In the same way, while some of us can create Sacred Space in the middle of the rush hour in Piccadilly Circus, others can do so only when the external surroundings and conditions are absolutely right for them. The following visualisation provides the opportunity to find out what works for you.

A Guided Visualisation: A Sacred Space

SCRIPT FOR THE GUIDE: *(To be read in a gentle trance-inducing voice.) Make yourself comfortable and close your eyes. Take a few deep breaths to help you relax. Feel the tension disappear stage by stage from the top of your head to the tips of your toes. Let your surroundings fade away as you gradually sink backwards through time and actuality and pass through the gateway of reality into the dreamtime. (When the participants are fully relaxed, begin the next stage.)*

Everybody needs a special kind of place, a retreat or a sanctuary, a place that feels safe and peaceful. If you were free to build this most wonderful place anywhere you like and had an unlimited amount of money to spend on it, what would it be like and where would it be located?

Your imagination can give you everything you're looking for. You have a minute of clock time, equal to all the time you need, to picture a suitable location and the design of your personal sanctuary....

Remember you can have anything you want in your sanctuary to make it the most wonderful place to be. You now have a minute of clock time, equal to all the time you need, to make a list of things that are important to you to include in your retreat....

You can create any barrier you think appropriate to exclude things or people that you might want to keep outside the sanctuary. This means that only those specifically invited in can gain entry....

The time has come now to return through the gateway you entered, back to your starting point. But remember you can come back to this space as often as you like and nobody can visit your sanctuary without an invitation because it belongs to only you.

Open your eyes now and stretch your arms and legs. Welcome back! Take a few minutes in silence to make some notes on the experiences you had on your journeys, which you can then share with the rest of the group/make a note of in your dream journal.

Sharing Sacred Space with Wolf

Sacred Mountain called to me
Eerie shades of pink and blue in the twilight
I climbed to a ledge by the mouth of a cave
And built myself a fire for warmth and comfort

Before long Wolf appeared
Cautiously skirting the area
Before accepting the offer of strips of meat
To share sacred space with me

Wolf howled at the moon
His way of connecting with the Great Mystery
And his source of power
To restore his balance and so his attraction

I watched, then followed his example
I stood, arms outstretched, and bathed in the moonbeams
So feeling part of the whole again
And released from my sense of alienation

Great Mystery
For as long as I feel I am part of you
I will never be alone
For you are my power source.

The Sun of Suns
[Reconciliation]

I If the Earth didn't revolve around the Sun, nothing could grow on this planet and you and I wouldn't be here. It's unfortunately something we tend to take for granted like many of the natural wonders of the world. But have you ever stopped to consider how the Sun came to be? Here's a story told by the Aboriginal peoples in Australia which offers an explanation.

How the Sun Came to Be

In the long ago Dreamtime the sun did not shine.

There was a young woman who decided to leave her group, because the elders would not allow her to marry the man of her choice. She would not listen to reason.

She went a long way away and hid in a dry, rocky area. There was little food here, and little water, and no good place to sleep; but hungry and thirsty and tired as she became, she still would not give up and return. Then she saw that the men from her group were coming to take her back by force, and she ran even further, into the most inaccessible part of the land.

Soon, torn and bruised by branches and rocks, she was exhausted and near to death, but somehow she summoned the energy to keep going. At last her ancestor spirits became so concerned that they lifted her gently away to a safe, quiet place in the sky world.

There she slept soundly for a long time. When she woke up she found plenty of food and water, and lit a camp fire. She was all alone but not afraid. Grateful that she was now warm and safe, she was still determined to live alone forever rather than return to her group.

At first she held on to her resentment towards her people. But as she looked down on them she saw that most of the men and women were sad that she had gone, and after a while her heart began to soften. Within a few days she found she was feeling quite homesick, but now she found that she belonged to the sky world and was no longer able to return.

"What shall I do?" she asked herself. "I cannot go back but I would like to help them." And then she saw a way in which she could help. Her people were cold. Occupied with all the chores of daily life, they could not sit by the camp fire and keep warm as she now could.

"J will build up my fire. J will make it so big that it will warm the busy people down below," she decided. All day she gave warmth to her people. As night came she let her fire die down, because then they were able to sit by their own camp fires.

When she saw that this helped and pleased her people, she made up her mind to light her fire every day. Soon her people began to look each day for her sky-world fire. All the people on earth became grateful for the warmth it gave them. They called it "the Sun".

The years were long for the young woman, exiled from her people forever, but the fact that she could shine her warmth on them each day brought her both joy and comfort.

Exercises for Teachers of English as a Foreign Language

Pre-listening: *If the Earth didn't revolve around the Sun, nothing could grow on this planet and you and I wouldn't be here. Working in small groups, make a list of all the uses we make of sunshine.*

Have you ever stopped to consider how the Sun came to be? Here's a story told by the Aboriginal peoples in Australia which offers an explanation.

Post-listening: Arrange the students in groups to make up stories for one of the following titles and circulate to provide any assistance required: "How The Moon Came To Be" or "How The Stars Came To Be". The students can then tell their stories to the rest of the class and produce them in written form for homework.

Once upon a time we had plenty of reasons to be thankful for the Sun but now we have reasons to fear it because of the damage we have done to the ozone layer. Fill each of the numbered gaps in the following passage with one suitable word.

Ozone is very damaging at ground…, (1) but … (2) the atmosphere it is absolutely critical … (3) maintaining … (4) on earth. The 'ozone layer' is a vast filter encircling the world, which … (5) us from the sun's potentially lethal…. (6) If the ultra-violet light … (7) reaches us is not filtered in this…, (8) it can … (9) serious eye disease and skin cancer. Recent evidence has … (10) that the ozone layer has been significantly … (11) by pollutants – particularly chlorofluorocarbons. CFCs are the propellants which … (12)

liquids and sprays from aerosol cans. They are also … (13) extensively in the fast food industry to make the insulating foam to … (14) food. It is an extraordinary … (15) that something as seemingly innocuous as a hairspray or a hamburger carton can pose such a serious … (16) to our environment, but the … (17) has been conclusively proved. CFCs float inexorably upwards and … (18) in the atmosphere for decades, gradually … (19) away at the ozone layer.

ANSWERS: 1. level 2. in 3. for 4. life 5. protects 6. rays 7. which 8. way 9. cause 10. shown 11. depleted 12. force 13. used 14. package 15. thought 16. threat 17. link 18. remain 19. eating

---

Whenever you ask people what they're frightened of, someone invariably says spiders. However, Native Americans welcome spiders into their homes because they are said to bring creativity into your life. They say that Spider wove the web that brought humans the first picture of the alphabet. The letters were part of the angles of her web. The following story is a Native American tale about the spider who rescued the animal kingdom from darkness. It also shows how we all have a part to play in the Great Mystery – all creatures great and small.

Grandmother Spider

In the beginning all was dark and the animal people bumped into each other, stumbling around in the darkness. They all wished there could be light. One day, when the animals felt they could not stand the situation any longer, they decided to get together to talk. Woodpecker said, "I have heard that there are people on the other side of the world who have light." The animals cheered as Woodpecker continued, "Maybe they will share some of their light with us."

Fox spoke up, "If they have it, they probably won't give any to us. If we want light we'll have to steal it."

Everyone began arguing about who should go. Each animal suggested someone who was strong, fast, intelligent or cunning. Possum spoke up, "I will go. I can hide the light under my fur." The animals agreed that he should go and off he went. As he travelled east the light grew so strong he had to screw up his eyes and even today, Possum's eyes are almost closed. When Possum arrived at the place of the light, he hid some of it in the fur of his bushy tail. It was so hot by the time he got home it had burned off all his fur which is why Possums have bare tails, even today. Possum arrived with no light.

The animals became discouraged when they saw Possum return empty-handed but Buzzard said, "I'll go. I will come back with the light." Buzzard flew so high the people of the light did not see him. He dived down, just as he does today, and caught a piece of the light and placed it on top of his head. The light was so hot it burned the top of his head and that is why, even today, buzzards are bald. Buzzard arrived with no light.

After two of the strongest, most responsible and determined animals failed, the others became even more upset. They sat around wondering what could be done. They moaned and groaned to each other, "Our brothers have done the best they could. Our finest have tried but we are still in darkness. What are we supposed to do now?"

Up piped a tiny voice, "Our men have done their best. Perhaps this is something a woman should try."

The animals looked around, trying to see the speaker. "Who is talking?" they asked.

"Grandmother Spider," she answered. "Although I am old, I have a plan. At least let me try. And if I fail you will not lose very much." The animals were sure she could not succeed but they agreed to give her a chance.

Grandmother Spider set to work. She fashioned a tiny bowl out of damp clay from the earth. She started east with her bowl, spinning her thread so that she would be able to find her way home again. When she got to the people of the light no one saw her because she was so small. She quickly took a tiny bit of the sun and put it into her bowl. Then she moved back along the thread she had spun. Even today, a spider's web looks like the rays of the sun.

When Grandmother Spider returned home with the light the animal people were amazed and overjoyed. "Thank you, Grandmother Spider," they said. "We will always honour you. We will never forget that you rescued us from the darkness, that you were the one to bring us light."

Sun worship was practised by the Iroquois, Plains, and Tsimshian peoples of North America and reached a high state of development among the Native Americans of Mexico and Peru. The sun was also a Hindu deity, considered to be evil by the Dravidians of southern India but to be benevolent by the Munda of the central parts. The Babylonians were sun worshippers, and in ancient Persia worship of the sun was an integral part of the elaborate cult of Mithras. The ancient Egyptians worshipped the sun god Ra.

In ancient Greece the deities of the sun were Helios and Apollo. The worship of Helios was widespread and on the island of Rhodes, in the Dodecanese, four white horses were sacrificed annually to the god. In time virtually all the functions of Helios were transferred to the god Apollo, in his identity as Phoebus. Sun worship persisted in Europe even after the introduction of Christianity and this can be seen from its disguised survival in such traditional Christian practices as the Easter bonfire and the Yule log at Christmas.

Jung wrote that "Man feels himself isolated in the cosmos. He is no longer involved in nature and has lost his emotional participation in natural events, which hitherto had a symbolic meaning for him…. His immediate communication with nature is gone forever, and the emotional energy it generated has sunk into the unconscious". It can be argued that the fragmentation to which we are subject is due to a disconnection from the source of life. It follows from this that our path to wholeness must involve a remembering of that self. As Rumi said, whoever has parted from his source longs to return to that state of union. The use of story as metaphor and guided visualisation can help to restore that link.

And now for a journey to the realms of the Upper World, via The Tree of Life to Mzetamze – the Sun of Suns in Georgian folklore, to reconnect with all that is.

A Guided Visualisation: To the Sun of Suns
SCRIPT FOR THE GUIDE: (To be read in a gentle trance-inducing voice.) Make yourself comfortable and close your eyes. Take a few deep breaths to help you relax. Breathe in the white light and breathe out all your tightness. Feel the tension disappear stage by stage from the top of your head to the tips of your toes. Let your surroundings fade away as you gradually sink backwards through time and actuality and pass through the gateway of reality into the dreamtime. (When the participants are fully relaxed, begin the next stage.)

You're standing at the foot of an enormous tree, which stretches up into the sky as far as the eyes can see. Choose the time of day you would like it to be and the season. Put your arms around the trunk of the tree and feel the texture of the bark. Be aware of the life-force flowing through it. Take a minute of clock time, equal to all the time you need, to enjoy the sensation, the feeling of the tree passing its strength on to you....

And now you start climbing the tree, using the branches for footholds, higher and higher you go, passing through the clouds on your way, higher and higher into a world of pure blue. And the higher you climb, the lighter you feel, as you leave all your worries and cares far behind you. Ahead of you, your destination is growing ever closer – Mzetamze, the Sun of Suns – where you're going to recharge your batteries.

The higher you climb, the hotter it gets as you start to approach Mzetamze. Find a suitable branch where you can rest for a while. Feel the warmth of the Sun of Suns' rays flow through your veins, carrying away all your aches and pains and filling you with an inexhaustible supply of energy. Take a minute of clock time, equal to all the time you need, to bathe in the healing sunlight and to appreciate your sense of oneness with all that is....

The time has now come for you to make your journey home again, back down the trunk of the tree, lowering yourself from branch to branch, filled with a new supply of energy to equip you for the journeys that lie ahead and all the special moments you have to look forward to. And as I count down slowly from ten, you lower yourself through the branches, down through the clouds, and back to the place you started from. 10 – 9 – 8 – 7 – 6 – 5 – 4 – 3 – 2 – 1 – and welcome home!

Open your eyes now and stretch your arms and legs. Take a few minutes in silence to make some notes on the experiences you had on your journeys, which you can then share with the rest of the group/make a note of in your dream journal.

Great
Smoking Mirror
[Leaving the Myth Behind]

Reality follows image and mental images can be regarded as blueprints upon which a corresponding condition or event will appear. Whatever we imagine, positive or negative, is magically attracted into our lives. We create our personal reality by the magic of the 'Law of Attraction'. Basically this law states that we create what we think about. Every single thought manifests itself in some reality and the more vivid the imagination and the firmer the expectation, the more likely it is to happen now.

Great Smoking Mirror is a widely used teaching of the Mayans. The Mayans stress that every life-form reflects every other life-form and that all originate from the same original source. If people would see all other human beings as unique expressions of themselves, there would be no basis for quarrelling or war. Great Smoking Mirror is all about leaving the myth behind. You are what you decide you are. Remove the smokescreen that hides your natural talents or worth, and stand tall.

The Great Smoking Mirror
Through the smoke
I see looking back
Another reflection of me

Mirror of my inner-self
Who are you
If I am me?

Mirror of my outer-self
What do others see?
Is the truth in my heart
Or human vanity?

— Jamie Sams, *Sacred Path Cards*

A Guided Visualisation: Great Smoking Mirror

SCRIPT FOR THE GUIDE: *(To be read in a gentle trance-inducing voice.) Make yourself comfortable and close your eyes. Take a few deep breaths to help you relax. Feel the tension disappear stage by stage from the top of your head to the tips of your toes. Let your surroundings fade away as you gradually sink backwards through time and actuality and pass through the gateway of reality into the dreamtime. (When the participants are fully relaxed, begin the next stage.)*

You find yourself walking along a pathway towards an isolated stone cottage. What time of day is it and what's the weather like? Small furry creatures scamper across the path in front of you, then back into the forest on your left. What are they and what do they tell you about the way that you're feeling? The pathway follows the course of a river. The river mirrors the course of your life up to now. What does it tell you? Take a minute of clock time, equal to all the time you need, to reflect on these matters....

You walk up the gravel path to the entrance of the cottage. You knock three times on the old wooden door and the doorkeeper welcomes you and ushers you inside. What does this person look like? How does this person behave towards you and how do you behave towards your host?

The wooden floorboards creak as you walk down the corridor towards the room at the end, the room it's now time for you to enter. Once inside, all you see is smoke and there is also the scent of incense. Gradually you get used to your surroundings and the smoke drifts away. You find yourself standing in front of a mirror, unlike any mirror you've ever seen before. The image facing you is blurred at first. Look into the mirror and see who you can really be. Gradually the image comes into focus. Take a minute of clock time, equal to all the time you need, to study your reflection – the reflection of your true potential, the person you were born to be....

Smoke fills the room and the mirror is obscured once again. The tim. come for you to make your journey home. You thank the doorkeeper giving you this unique opportunity and the heavy wooden door is closed behind you. And as you walk back along the pathway, what changes to your surroundings do you notice? Back you walk along the pathway, the forest to your right, the river to your left, back, back, the same way you came, back, back, through the dreamtime, back into this reality and back to the place you started from.

Open your eyes now and stretch your arms and legs. Welcome home! Take a few minutes in silence to make some notes on the experiences you had on your journeys, which you can then share with the rest of the group/make a note of in your dream journal.

Heart Knowing chant

Help me to see
The face of me.
Help me to hear
The voice of me.

Help me to know
The heart of me.
Help me to be
The spirit of me.

— Anasazi chant

The
Stone People

[Communing with the Record Keepers]

In the world of the shaman, other beings, natural objects and the universe itself are all endowed with vital essence or soul, and the shaman attempts to communicate with these sources to alleviate suffering. What I like about the story presented below is the way in which the pebbles are endowed with life by Ben Adam in his game. It is remarkable to observe what pleasure children can derive from the little things in life with the help of their imaginations or inner resources. However, the natural ease with which young people can enter other realities is frequently frowned upon by their teachers and parents and regarded as childish, so the facility is discouraged and quickly lost. Hopefully, with the emerging interest in right-brain learning, more and more adults will come to see the value of such experience and be motivated to relearn the skill.

The Pebble People

Ben Adam sat outside his grandparents' weathered old loghouse.

He liked to sit outside and listen to the sounds of the forest. Especially after one of his grandma's famous chicken and dumpling dinners. And he liked to play one of his favourite games – making rocks war dance. So he started looking for different-coloured pebbles. Some were easily scraped off the surface of the well-worn path to the grandparents' loghouse, others he had to dig and scratch out of the earth.

Finally, he found the ones he wanted – black ones, white ones, red ones, yellow ones, and blue ones. Holding the pebbles on an open palm, Ben Adam talked to them. He spoke to the pebbles for a long time about the respect and the discipline they should have while wearing the traditional clothing the Creator had given them. He talked of the symbols the old people said were in their dress. He spoke of how they should all try to conduct themselves with dignity. Ben Adam repeated the words of an uncle who had helped him dress for a war dance sometime before.

After several moments of serious meditation, he placed the pebbles on the bottomside of an overturned tin bucket, each according to its own size and colour. He carefully placed the red, yellow, blue, white, and black pebbles into the circular grooves of the bucket in the formation of a bustle, the middlemost circle being the drum. Under his

117

breath, he sang the ancient words of his favourite war dance song, but he didn't drum yet because he didn't want the dancers moved.

Ben Adam finished his silent song and again spoke to the pebbles. His message contained a prayer of thanksgiving that his people were alive to see another day and that this day was a day they had chosen to come together in celebration of tribal customs. He thanked all the dancers, drummers, and spectators. He asked the Creator to bestow special blessings upon them throughout the evening and as each of them travelled back to their homes.

Ben Adam asked for blessings on behalf of people who were sick and could not attend the dance. He prayed for those imprisoned by steel bars and by personal weaknesses. And he asked the people to remember those people who had died since the last time they had gathered. Ben Adam's words were very well selected and presented to the pebble people.

Following a moment of silence, he started singing a warm-up song. He drummed slowly on the bottomside ridge of the battered old bucket and watched proudly as the pebbles began to dance. At first they moved slowly about the grooves of the bucket according to the rhythm of the song. "For this slow beat the traditional dancers should be thankful," Ben Adam said.

The pace quickened. Ben Adam sang louder and drummed faster. The dancers hopped about fervently, like fancy dancers, their thunderous hoofbeats in tune with the drumming and their blurred colours lit the air. Some of the pebbles began falling off the edge of the bucket to the ground. Ben Adam drummed and sang as long as there were some pebble dancers left.

After only a few were left, Ben Adam announced to them, "This will be a contest song!" He drummed faster and faster and harder until all the pebbles fell off the bucket. Then, carefully, he picked up those that were the last to fall. "Gee, that was a good contest," he said.

He thanked the dancers and said, "One day there will be a big, big contest. Only those who are really good can come and participate in it." Ben Adam put the winning pebbles into marked jars to save. "The winners of the contest and my favourite dancers I will take into the house and put away in my fishtank for the winner," he said to himself and the pebble people.

– Roger Jack, *Earth Power Coming*

A Guided Visualisation: The Record Keeper

SCRIPT FOR THE GUIDE: *(To be read in a gentle, trance-inducing voice.) Make yourself comfortable and close your eyes. Take a few deep breaths to help you relax. Feel the tension disappear, stage by stage, from the top of your head to the tips of your toes. Let your surroundings fade away as you gradually sink backwards through time and actuality and pass through the gateway of reality into the dreamtime. (When the participants are fully relaxed, begin the next stage.)*

You're walking along a beach by the sea in the sunshine. Hear the sound of the waves, feel the sand between your toes and taste the salt on your lips. You stop still for a moment to enjoy the experience. Now you slowly start to walk again and see in front of you an interesting pebble lying on the ground. You slowly reach down and pick it up and notice how good it feels in your hand. Now you say these words to it:

> *Record Keeper of the Earth*
> *Will you please explain*
> *The history that gave me birth*
> *The truth you do contain*
> *Record Holder of the Earth*
> *Please bring me new awareness*
> *Of where I come from*
> *And where I'm going.*

Take a minute of clock time, equal to all the time you need, to receive the answers to your questions....

You return the pebble to the place where you found it and stand still for a moment. And as you stand there and watch, you feel the sun on your back and see the waves coming in, slowly washing over your pebble, so very slowly, bit by bit, until it's totally submerged and lost among all the others. And you feel happy inside because you know the answers now. It's so beautiful watching the waves, so very relaxing, a moment in time you will never forget.

And now it's time to return, back the same way you came, back to the place where you started. And as you walk back along the sandy beach, you're smiling because you're still enjoying everything you've seen, heard, felt, smelled and tasted. And all these beautiful things you take back with you. Whenever you want or need, you can just return and enjoy this special place again.

Now take three slow, deep breaths, and each time blow the air out so you can hear yourself exhale. Breathe in the light, and breathe out all your tightness.... Breathe in the light, and breathe out all your tightness.... Breathe in the light and breathe out all your tightness. Now open your eyes and smile at someone!

Stretch your arms and legs. Take a few minutes in silence to make some notes on the experiences you had on your journey, which you can then share with the rest of the group/make a note of in your dream journal.

Stone Person

Perhaps
When you tire of your surroundings
You will a child to pick you up
And move to another location

Or perhaps your mantra is the tide
Forever washing over and being sucked from under you
And you've long since reached enlightenment.

Seen Through the Eyes of a Stone Person

Please excuse my laughter
It's meant without any disrespect
But the petty problems
Which seem to be of such magnitude
To you at the moment
(Just a step in the learning process)
On time will leave a mark
That will barely scratch my surface
So see them through my eyes
And you'll be laughing with me too.

The Wildman & the Sea

[The Circularity of Time]

Talking with the Water

The ebb and flow of the tide is relentless
Just like the waxing and the waning of the moon
Coming in and going out, the rhythm of life
Honour the natural order and attune to it
To let go of your old life and let in the new
By trusting in the certainty of the process
Instead of locking yourself up in a casket
And then endlessly moaning about the lost key.

In non-ordinary reality, a minute of clock time can last forever. You discover the circularity as well as the linearity of time, acting both in history as well as in the depth of the world of timelessness. The story from Japan that follows explores this concept: Urashima is given the opportunity to shift out of limited consciousness and gain access to the great workings of the timeless world. However, as he ultimately discovers, there is a price to pay for this gift.

Urashima

Many years ago a boy lived down by the sea, where the great green waves came riding in to break on the shore in clouds of salty spray. This boy, Urashima, loved the water as a brother, and was out in his boat every day and in all weathers, from dawn to dusk. One day as he was fishing, something tugged at his line, and he pulled it in. It was not a fish, as he expected, but a wrinkled old turtle.

"Well," said Urashima, "if I cannot get a fish for my dinner, at least I will not keep this old fellow from all the dinners he still has to come." For in Japan they say that all the turtles live to be a thousand years old.

So the kind-hearted Urashima tumbled him back into the water, and what a splash he made! But from the spray there seemed to rise a beautiful girl who stepped into the boat with Urashima. She said to him: "I am the daughter of the sea-god. I was that turtle you just threw back into the water. My father sent me to see if you were as kind as you seemed, and I see that you are. We who live under the water say that those who love the sea can never be unkind. Will you come with us to the dragon palace far below the green waves?"

Urashima was very glad to go, so each took an oar and away they sped.

Long before the sun had sunk below the horizon, Urashima and the Dragon Princess had reached the twilight depths of the ocean. The fishes scudded about them through branches of coral and trailing ropes of seaweed. The roar of the waves about came to them only as a trembling murmur, to make the silence sweeter.

Here was the dragon palace of seashell and pearl, of coral and emerald. It gleamed with all the thousand lights and tints that lurk in the depths of the water. Fishes with silver fins were ready to come at their wish. The daintiest foods that the ocean holds for her children were served to them. Their waiters were seven dragons, each with a golden tail.

Urashima lived in a dream of happiness with the Dragon Princess for four short years. Then he remembered his home, and longed to see his family and friends once again. He wished to see the village streets and the wave-lapped stretch of sand where he used to play.

He did not need to tell the princess of his wish, for she knew it all, and said: "I see that you long for your home once more; I will not keep you, but I fear to have you go. Still, I know you wish to come back, so take this box and let nothing happen to it, for if it is opened, you can never return."

She then placed him in his boat and the lapping waves bore him up and away until his prow crunched on to the sand where he used to play.

Around that bend in the bay stood his father's cottage, close by the great pine tree. But as he came nearer he saw neither tree nor house. He looked around. The houses he could see looked unfamiliar. Strange children were peering at him and strange people walked the streets. He wondered at the change in four short years.

An old man came along the shore and Urashima spoke to him.

"Can you tell me, sir, where the cottage of Urashima has gone?"

"Urashima?" said the old man. "Urashima! Why, don't you know that he was drowned four hundred years ago, while out fishing? His brothers, their children, and their children's children have all lived and died since then. Four hundred years ago it was, on a summer day like this, they say."

Gone! His father and mother, his brothers and playmates, and the cottage he loved so well. How he longed to see them; but he must hurry back to the dragon palace, for now that was his only home. But how should he go? He walked along the shore, but could not remember the way to take. Forgetting the promise he had made to the Princess, he took out the little pearl box and opened it. From it a white cloud seemed to rise, and as it floated away he thought he saw the face of the Dragon Princess. He called to her, reached for her, but the cloud was already floating far out over the waves.

As it floated away he suddenly seemed to grow old. His hands shook and his hair turned white. He seemed to be melting away to join the past in which he had lived.

When the new moon hung her horn of light in the branches of the pine tree, there was only a small pearl box on the sandy rim of shore, and the great green waves were lifting white arms of foam as they had done four hundred years before.

Exercises for Teachers of English as a Foreign Language

Pre-listening: Elicit what a 'mermaid' is from the class, then brainstorm what the students associate mermaids with and board the language that comes up in the form of a mind map. A mind map is a non-linear form of note taking which links key words and ideas. In its simplest form, it could consist of the word MERMAIDS inside a circle in the centre of the board, with arrows radiating from the circumference pointing to key vocabulary. An alternative would be to stick up a picture of a mermaid in the centre of the board.

Post-listening: Time Idioms. The students can work in pairs on this matching activity, and the first pair to finish can board their answers – the numbers and the letters – for the rest of the class to see whether they agree or not. Alternatively, the idioms and the explanations can be copied onto individual cards. Give everyone in the room either a number or a letter, and invite them to find their missing halves. This can be an effective way of shuffling the pairings as the learners then sit and work with their new partners. It is also appreciated by the kinaesthetic students – those who learn through movement.

TIME IDIOMS. Match the idioms on the left with the explanations on the right. There are more explanations than you need so make sure you select the correct ones!

1. You'll just have to bide your time.
2. You don't seem to know the time of day.
3. I think you're just playing for time.
4. You're taking your time, aren't you?
5. There's no time like the present.
6. You seem to be having the time of your life.
7. You're clearly ahead of your times.
8. You seem to have a lot of time on your hands.
9. Time and tide wait for no man.
10. There's a time and a place for everything.

a. Do it now rather than later.
b. I can see that you're really enjoying yourself.
c. It's clear you know nothing at all.
d. It seems that you're trying to delay things.
e. It's time you got a move on.
f. Take advantage of the chances you get.
g. You're always late for everything.
h. You're not taking the game seriously enough.
i. You don't appear to be very occupied.
j. You need to be patient.

k. You seem to be taking ages to finish the job.
l. You should have been born in an earlier period of history.
m. Your ideas are too modern to be fully understood.
n. Your behaviour is unsuitable in the present situation.

Answers: 1 – j, 2 – c , 3 – d, 4 – e, 5 – a, 6 – b, 7 – m, 8 – i, 9 – f, 10 – n.

You can then arrange the learners in groups of four to write a short story or a dialogue incorporating as many of the idioms as they can. The group who include the most idioms can be given a prize. Alternatively, the students could take it in turns to mime one of the idioms for the others to guess.

The matching activity based on the collocations that appear in the story can be used in the review stage of the lesson to help reinforce the new expressions introduced in the text.

Without looking back at the story, match the adjectives on the left with the nouns on the right to complete the collocations:

1. daintiest	a. dawn
2. lapping	b. depths
3. new	c. evening
4. purple	d. fins
5. russet	e. foods
6. salty	f. moon
7. silver	g. spray
8. twilight	h. waves

Answers: 1 – e, 2 – h, 3 – f, 4 – a, 5 – c, 6 – g, 7 – d, 8 – b.

What other stories do you know about sea-gods or monsters who live under the water? You can invite the students to produce a written account of one for homework.

A Guided Visualisation: The Old Man of the Sea

SCRIPT FOR THE GUIDE: (To be read in a gentle trance-inducing voice.) Make yourself comfortable and close your eyes. Take a few deep breaths to help you relax. Feel the tension disappear stage by stage from the top of your head to the tips of your toes. Let your surroundings fade away as you gradually sink backwards through time and actuality and pass through the gateway of this reality into the dreamtime. (When the participants are fully relaxed, begin the next stage.)

Ahead of you there's an entrance to a cave and you bend down low to enter it. Inside you find a pile of branches covering the way into a tunnel. You slide down the tunnel to find yourself in a passageway lit by candles leading out to the sea. You wade out purposefully into the water, secure in the knowledge that nothing can harm you because the Old Man of the Sea, Neptune, is calling to you.

You follow a pathway of rocks along the seabed towards a cloud of light ahead of you. There you find three steps leading up to a golden throne covered with seaweed and Neptune waiting for you. You have a minute of clock time, equal to all the time you need, to study the scene before you....

"I knew you'd come and I've been expecting you. I've called you here to give you guidance, to help you with the question that's been on your mind and that you've come here to find an answer to." You have a minute of clock time, equal to all the time you need, to ask and hear the answer to your question....

"Before you leave I have a personal gift to give you, something to help you on your future path through life and to remind you of our meeting." You have a minute of clock time, equal to all the time you need, to appreciate the special gift....

You thank the Old Man of the Sea and say goodbye before setting off on your journey back, remembering to take your special gift with you. You follow the pathway back along the seabed, emerging from the water to enter the passageway lit by candles. You pull yourself up through the tunnel, cover the entrance with branches to keep it hidden, and make your way out of the mouth of the cave, back to the place you started from. Welcome home.

Open your eyes now and stretch your arms and legs. Welcome home! Take a few minutes in silence to make some notes on the experiences you had on your journeys, which you can then share with the rest of the group/make a note of in your dream journal.

It is said that a merman was caught by fishermen from Orford in Suffolk during the reign of Henry II (1154 – 1189) and the following tale is based on this story. Fear of the unknown can lead us to reject or even attempt to destroy what we come across when it does not fit into the map of reality we have chosen to adopt. The Wildman is a metaphor for what lies beyond our limited vision and our attitude towards it.

The Wildman

Don't ask me my name. I've heard you have names. I have no name.

They say this is how I was born. A great wave bored down a river, and at the mouth of the river it ran up against a great wave of the sea. The coupled waves kicked like legs and whirled like arms and swayed like hips; sticks in the water snapped like bones and the seaweed bulged like gristle and muscle. In this way the waves rose. When they fell, I was there.

My home is water as your home is earth. I rise to the surface to breathe air, I glide down through the darkening rainbow. The water sleeks my hair as I swim. And when I stand on the sea-bed, the currents comb my waving hair, my whole body seems to ripple.

Each day I go to the land for food. I swim to the shore, but I'm careful not to be seen. Small things, mice, shrews, moles, I like them to eat. I snuffle and grub through the growth and undergrowth and grab them, and squeeze the warm blood out of them, and chew them.

Always before sunset I'm back in the tugging, chuckling, sobbing water. Then the blue darkness that comes down over the sea comes inside me too. I feel heavy until morning. If I stayed too long on the land I might be found, lying there, heavy, unable even to drag myself back to the water.

My friends are seals. They dive as I do, and swim as I do. Their hair is like my hair. I sing songs with their little ones. They've shown me their secret place, a dark grotto so deep that I howled for the pain of the water pressing round me there and rose to the surface, gasping for air. My friends are the skimming plaice and the flickering eel and the ticklish trout. My friends are all the fishes.

As I swam near the river mouth, something caught my legs and tugged at them. I tried to push it away with my hands and it caught my hands and my arms too. I kicked; I flailed; I couldn't escape. I was dragged through the water, up out of the darkness into the indigo, the purple, the pale blue. I was lifted into the air, the sunlight, and down into a floating thing.

Others. There were others in it, others, others as I am. But their faces were not covered with hair. They had very little hair I could see except on their heads, but they were covered with animal skins and furs. When they saw me they were afraid and trembled and backed away and one fell into the water.

I struggled and bit but I was caught in the web they had made. They took me to land and a great shoal gathered round me there. Then they carried me in that web to a great high place of stone and tipped me out into a gloomy grotto.

One of them stayed by me and kept making noises. I couldn't understand him. I could tell he was asking me things. I would like to have
asked him things. How were you born? Why do you have so little hair?
Why do you live on land? I looked at him, I kept looking at him, and
when the others came back, I looked at them: their hairless hands,
their legs, their shining eyes. There were so many of them almost like
me, and I've never once seen anyone in the sea like me.

They brought me two crossed sticks. Why? What are they? They
pushed them into my face, they howled at me. One of them smacked
my face with his hand. Why was that? It hurt. Then another with long
pale hair came and wept tears over me. I licked my lips; the tears
tasted like the sea. Was this one like me? Did this one come from the
sea? I put my arms round its waist but it shrieked and pushed me
away.

They brought me fish to eat. I wouldn't eat fish. Later they brought
me meat; I squeezed it until it was dry and then I ate it.

I was taken out into sunlight, down to the river mouth. The rippling,
rippling water. It was pink and lilac and grey; I shivered with
longing at the sight of it. I could see three rows of nets spread across
the river from bank to bank. Then they let me go, they let me dive into
the water. It coursed through my long hair. I laughed and passed
under the first net and the second net and the third net. I was free.
But why am I only free away from those who are like me, with those
who are not like me? Why is the sea my home?

They were all shouting and waving their arms, and jumping up and
down at the edge of the water. They were all calling out across the
grey wavelets. Why? Did they want me to go back after all? Did they
want me to be their friend?

I wanted to go back, I wanted them as friends. So I stroked back
under the nets again and swam to the sandy shore. They fell on me
then, and twisted my arms, and hurt me. I howled. I screamed. They
tied long webs round me and more tightly round me, and carried me
back to the place of stone, and threw me into the gloomy grotto.

I bit through the webs. I slipped through the window bars. It was almost night and the blue heaviness was coming into me. I staggered away, back to the water, the waiting dark water.

– Kevin Crossley-Holland, *British Folk Tales*

The Dream Cushion

[Differentiating between Needs and Wants]

A lot of the mountains we aspire to climb are beyond our reach or are not worth climbing in the first place. By looking within we can find out which of our dreams are truly worth pursuing. We can also learn to appreciate what we already have instead of taking it for granted. It is also important to differentiate between needs and wants because there's a world of difference between the two. *Need* implies the object of your desire is essential for your survival but you can count what you genuinely need on the fingers of one hand. *Want* implies the object of your desire is non-essential and you can live without it. By reformulating 'I need' statements into 'I want' statements life becomes a lot more manageable. The stories and the visualisations that follow explore these issues. It soon becomes evident that we need to give more thought to the language we use, its implications and consequences.

The Stonecutter

Once upon a time there lived a stonecutter, who went every day to a great rock in the side of a big mountain and cut out slabs for gravestones or for houses. He understood very well the kinds of stones wanted for the different purposes, and as he was a careful workman he had plenty of customers. For a long time he was quite happy and contented, and asked for nothing better than what he had.

Now in the mountain dwelt a spirit, which now and then appeared to men, and helped them in many ways to become rich and prosperous. The stonecutter, however, had never seen this spirit, and only shook his head, with an unbelieving air, when anyone spoke of it. But a time was coming when he would learn to change his opinion.

One day the stonecutter carried a gravestone to the house of a rich man, and saw there all sorts of beautiful things, of which he had never even dreamed. Suddenly his daily work seemed to grow harder and heavier, and he said to himself: "Oh, if only I were a rich man, and could sleep in a bed with silken curtains and golden tassels, how happy I should be!"

And a voice answered him: "Your wish is heard; a rich man you shall be!"

At the sound of the voice the stonecutter looked round, but could see nobody. He thought it was all his fancy, and picked up his tools and went home, for he did not feel inclined to do any more work that day. But when he reached the little house where he lived, he stood still with amazement, for instead of his wooden hut was a stately palace filled with splendid furniture, and most splendid of all was the bed, in every respect like the one he had envied. He was nearly beside himself with joy, and in his new life the old one was soon forgotten.

It was now the beginning of summer, and each day the sun blazed more fiercely. One morning the heat was so great that the stonecutter could scarcely breathe, and he determined he would stop at home till the evening. He was rather dull, for he had never learned how to amuse himself, and was peeping through the closed blinds to see what was going on in the street, when a little carriage passed by, drawn by servants dressed in blue and silver. In the carriage sat a prince, and over his head a golden umbrella was held, to protect him from the sun's rays.

"Oh, if I were only a prince!" said the stonecutter to himself, as the carriage vanished round the corner. "Oh, if I were only a prince, and could go in such a carriage and have a golden umbrella held over me, how happy I should be!"

And the voice of the mountain spirit answered: "Your wish is heard; a prince you shall be!"

And a prince he was. Before his carriage rode one company of men and another behind it; servants dressed in scarlet and gold bore him along, the coveted umbrella was held over his head, everything his heart could desire was his. But yet it was not enough. He looked round still for something to wish for, and when he saw that in spite of the water he poured on his grass the rays of the sun scorched it, and that in spite of the umbrella held over his head each day his face grew browner and browner, he cried in his anger; "The sun is mightier than I; oh, if I were only the sun!"

And the mountain spirit answered: "Your wish is heard; the sun you shall be."

And the sun he was, and he felt himself proud in his power. He shot his beams above and below, on earth and in heaven; he burned up the grass in the fields and scorched the faces of princes as well as of poorer folk. But in a short time he began to grow tired of his might, for there seemed nothing left for him to do. Discontent once more filled his soul, and when a cloud covered his face, and hid the earth from him, he cried in his anger: "Does the cloud hold captive my rays, and is it mightier than I? Oh, that I were a cloud, and mightier than any!"

And the mountain spirit answered: "Your wish is heard; a cloud you shall be!"

And a cloud he was, and lay between the sun and the earth. He caught the sun's beams and held them, and to his joy the earth grew green again and flowers blossomed. But that was not enough for him, and for days and weeks he poured forth rain till the rivers overflowed their banks, and the crops of rice stood in water. Towns and villages were destroyed by the power of the rain, only the great rock on the mountainside remained unmoved. The cloud was amazed at the sight, and cried in wonder. "Is the rock, then, mightier than I? Oh, if I were only the rock!"

And the mountain spirit answered: "Your wish is heard; the rock you shall be!"

And the rock he was, and gloried in his power. Proudly he stood, and neither the heat of the sun nor the force of the rain could move him. "This is better than all!" he said to himself. But one day he heard a strange noise at his feet, and when he looked down to see what it could be, he saw a stonecutter driving tools into his surface. Even while he looked a trembling feeling ran all through him, and a great block broke off and fell upon the ground. Then he cried in his wrath: "Is a mere child of earth mightier than a rock? Oh, if I were only a man!"

And the mountain spirit answered: "Your wish is heard. A man once more you shall be!"

And a man he was, and in the sweat of his brow he toiled again at his trade of stonecutting. His bed was hard and his food scanty, but he had learned to be satisfied with it, and did not long to be something or somebody else. And as he never asked for things he had not got, or desired to be greater and mightier than other people, he was happy at last, and heard the voice of the mountain spirit no longer.

– *Best-loved Folktales of the World* selected by Joanna Cole

A Guided Visualisation: A Meeting with Amirani

SCRIPT FOR THE GUIDE: (To be read in a gentle trance-inducing voice.) Make yourself comfortable and close your eyes. Take a few deep breaths to help you relax. Feel the tension disappear stage by stage from the top of your head to the tips of your toes. Let your surroundings fade away as you gradually sink backwards through time and actuality and pass through the gateway of reality into the dreamtime. (When the participants are fully relaxed, begin the next stage.)

We all find ourselves in situations we can't escape from for one reason or another – living with difficult relatives, boring jobs that have to be done, studying for exams – the list, in fact is endless. Take a minute of clock time, equal to all the time you need, to reflect now on your own situation and the ties that bind you....

Who can we turn to for help in such circumstances, to show us the patience we need to put up with our difficulties? The answer, of course is Amirani, son of the goddess Dali, chained to the rocks until the end of time, and today you're going on a journey to meet him.

You're walking along a winding path in the foothills of the Caucasus. Breathe the fresh mountain air and hear the sound of the birds flying high overhead. You can't see what's round the next corner because the path twists and turns all the time. Eventually you turn to the right, and there you find Amirani, lying against the face of a rock, with chains around his wrists and ankles and his faithful dog sitting by his side. You have a minute of clock time, equal to all the time you need, to introduce yourself to Amirani and tell him what's troubling you. And you can be sure that he'll be patient with you because he's grateful to have some company....

"However difficult your problems are," Amirani says "they can't be as bad as mine. How would you feel about being chained to a rock until the end of time? Try to see the positive side of your situation instead of just the negative." Take a minute of clock time, equal to all the time you need, to focus on everything you have reason to be thankful for and this will surely make you feel a lot better....

And now the time has come for you to make your journey home. Thank Amirani for the help he's given you and look around for a gift you can leave him to show your appreciation. You have a minute of clock time, equal to all the time you need, to choose something appropriate....

Turn your back on the scene and start to make your way back, back along the same pathway through the foothills, back through time and actuality, back through the gateway that marks the boundary between the two worlds and back to the place you started from.

Take a deep breath and then let it out. Open your eyes and smile at the first person you see. Stretch your arms and legs, then stamp your feet on the ground to make sure you're really back. Take a few minutes in silence to make some notes on the experiences you had on your journeys, which you can then share with the rest of the group/make a note of in your dream journal.

Happiness means different things to different people – having loads of money for some, watching a beautiful sunset for others. What is happiness for you? The following story is about the happiest man in the world and it comes to you all the way from Uzbekistan. If peace of mind eludes you, perhaps the solution is close at hand, staring at you in the face, as it is for the man in the story.

The Happiest Man in the World

A man who was living in comfortable enough circumstances, went one day to see a certain sage, reputed to know everything. He said to him:

"Great sage, I have no material problems. In fact, I'm quite well off. But for some reason I just can't seem to find peace of mind. For years I've tried to be happy, to come to terms with the world, but the answer still eludes me. What can I do to be cured of this malaise?"

The sage answered: "My friend, what's hidden to some is apparent to others. Again, what's apparent to some is hidden to others. I have the cure for your condition, though it's no ordinary medication you can buy in a chemist's. You must set out on your travels, seeking the happiest man in the world. And as soon as you find him, you must ask him for his shirt and put it on."

This seeker thereupon restlessly started looking for happy men. One after another he found them and questioned them. Again and again they said: "Yes, I am happy, but there's one even happier than me." After travelling through one country after another for many, many days, he found the wood in which everyone said lived the happiest man in the world.

He heard the sound of laughter coming from among the trees and quickened his step until he came upon a man sitting in a glade.

"Are you the happiest man in the world, as people say?" he asked.

"Certainly I am," said the other man.

"My name is so-and-so, my condition is such-and-such, and my remedy, ordered by the greatest sage, is to wear your shirt. Please give it to me and I'll give you anything I have in exchange."

The happiest man looked at him closely, and he laughed. He laughed and he laughed and he laughed. When he had quietened down a little, the restless man, rather annoyed at this reaction, said:

"Why are you laughing at me? Is there something wrong with you?"

"Perhaps," said the happiest man, "but if you'd only taken the trouble to look, you'd have seen that I don't possess a shirt."

"So what am I to do now?"

"Now you will finally be cured. Striving for something unattainable provides the means to achieve what is needed. It's like when a man gathers all his strength to jump across a stream as if it were far wider than it really is. The result is that he gets across the stream." The happiest man in the world then took off the turban he'd been wearing that had concealed his face. The restless man saw that he was none other than the great sage who had originally advised him.

"But why didn't you tell me all this years ago, when I came to see you?" the restless man asked in puzzlement.

"Because you weren't ready then to understand. You needed certain experiences first, and they had to be given to you in a manner which would ensure that you learnt from them."

A Guided Visualisation: Sizmara the Dreamer

SCRIPT FOR THE GUIDE (To be read in a gentle trance-inducing voice.) Make yourself comfortable and close your eyes. Take a few deep breaths to help you relax. Breathe in the white light and breathe out all your tightness. Feel the tension disappear stage by stage from the top of your head to the tips of your toes. Let your surroundings fade away as you gradually sink backwards through time and actuality and pass through the gateway of reality into the dreamtime. (When the participants are fully relaxed, begin the next stage.)

We describe ourselves as poor when we've got no money but our dreams can make us rich. Sizmara, a simple peasant from a village in Imereti, knew all about this and today's a special day in your life because you're going to have the chance to meet him. Take a minute of clock time, equal to all the time you need, to ask yourself what kind of dreams you'd like to have....

And now you're walking through the main street of Sizmara's village. Feel the heat of the midday sun beating down on you, hear the cock-a-doodle-doo, and be careful not to step on the chickens pecking for food around your feet. You sit down under the shade of a tree by the roadside to take a breather. And you have a minute of clock time, equal to all the time you need, to enjoy the sights, sounds and smells of the village....

Your thoughts are interrupted by a young man who walks towards you, wearing a colourful headband. "My name's Sizmara and I can help you to dance your dreams awake." He removes his headband and ties it around your forehead. And you have a minute of clock time, equal to all the time you need, to see your dreams for the future unfold....

"And now the moment has come for me to remove the magical headband because your time with me has come to an end. But remember that as long as you trust in the process, you have the power to turn your dreams into reality and you must make sure you never forget this." ....

You thank Sizmara for showing you the way forward and start to make your way home again, back through the village the same way you came, back, back, through time and actuality, back through the gateway between the two worlds and back to the place you started from. Welcome home!...

Open your eyes now and stretch your arms and legs. Take a few minutes in silence to make some notes on the experiences you had on your journeys, which you can then share with the rest of the group/make a note of in your dream journal.

A Guided Visualisation: The Goddess Nana

SCRIPT FOR THE GUIDE: *(To be read in a gentle trance-inducing voice.) Make yourself comfortable and close your eyes. Take a few deep breaths to help you relax. Feel the tension disappear stage by stage from the top of your head to the tips of your toes. Let your surroundings fade away as you gradually sink backwards through time and actuality and pass through the gateway of reality into the dreamtime. (When the participants are fully relaxed, begin the next stage.)*

We all have times in our lives when we feel stuck in a rut, having to face the same old boring routine day after day, times when we hunger for something new and exciting to make life worth living again. Take a minute of clock time, equal to all the time you need, to reflect now on your own situation and to consider what you would like to plant for your future....

Who can we turn to for help to make the seeds we plant grow, to help us to dance our dreams awake? The answer, of course, is Nana, the goddess of fertility. So wrap your seeds up carefully in a bundle because today you're going on a journey to meet her!

It's springtime and you're standing in a field on a warm sunny day. A shower of beautiful sunlight pours down over you from head to foot, bathing you in a gentle, calming warmth. Smell the sweet scent of the flowers all round you, hear the buzzing of the bees and the sound of the birds, and feel the earth beneath your bare feet. You have a minute of clock time, equal to all the time you need, to enjoy this special moment....

From nowhere the most beautiful and enchanting woman appears and gently approaches you. You find it impossible to take your eyes off her and she glows with a radiance not of this world. She reaches out and takes your hand. Her voice is gentle and soothing. "My name is the goddess Nana and I've called you here to offer you my help. Tell me what your dreams for the future are and I will plant the seeds for you and help them to grow." You have a minute of clock time, equal to all the time you need, to tell Nana what your dreams are and to listen to the advice she has to give you....

"Although you will see me no more, whenever you need me I'll be by your side to help make your dreams a reality. And if your belief is strong enough, then anything is possible."

Just as suddenly as Nana appeared, she leaves you and a rainbow in the sky takes her place. Pick some flowers to take back home with you to remind you of your meeting, for now the time has come to return again. And back you travel, through time and actuality, back through the gateway that marks the boundary between the two worlds, back to the place you started from. And you return with renewed confidence in your ability to achieve what you want, determined to let nothing stand in your way, secure in the knowledge that you'll never be alone and that Nana will always be by your side to help you.

Take a deep breath and then let it out slowly. Open your eyes and smile at the first person you see. Stretch your arms and legs, then stamp your feet on the ground to make sure you're really home. Take a few minutes in silence to make some notes on the experiences you had on your journeys, which you can then share with the rest of the group/make a note of in your dream journal.

In many traditions dreams are regarded not only as "the royal road to the unconscious," to quote Freud, but also the royal road to wisdom and awakening. Moreover, the dreaming we do while awake is seen to be just as important as that which we do while asleep. In our daydreams we replay the past and prepare for the future, entertaining possibilities and practising new options. Journeying offers similar possibilities. Jung recognised the importance of these waking dreams and was no doubt influenced by the time he spent with the Plains Indians in the early 1930s.

The Native Americans had a complex system of categorising dreams according to their importance. In the Choctaw tradition, for example, there are four kinds of sleeping dreams – property dreams that foretell the receiving of material possessions, no-account dreams which are considered to be too ambiguous to have any real meaning, wish dreams which express our hopes, and medicine dreams which bring such a powerful vision that we feel compelled to dance it awake.

An illustration of the transformational power of dreams can be found in the following story. By making use of our intrapersonal skills, we can learn a great deal from both our sleeping and waking dreams and it is well worth keeping a journal on your bedside table for the purpose. They say that if you hang an owl's feather over your bed at night it helps you to recall what you dreamt about when you wake up.

The Dream Cushion

Somewhere to the north in a mountainous land, there lived a warrior king who had a magical cushion. If he slept on the pillow and dreamed about something, he could change it into whatever he wanted. The cushion had been a gift from a tradesman he jailed for not paying his tax. After the tradesman's release from prison, he handed the pillow to the warrior king and said, smiling, "Be careful what you wish for in your dreams."

If the warrior king dreamed about an ordinary rock, he could change the rock into pure gold, which he would use to buy food and weapons for his armies. And if he dreamed about a mouse, it would become a mighty stallion, which he would ride into battle.

The warrior king had everything he wanted. He would ride for miles about his kingdom and admire all he ruled. He would glory in the victory of battle. He would sit in his counting house and count all his money. As the years passed, however, he began to notice an emptiness that could not be filled with the thrill of a victorious defeat of his enemies, or the taking of lands by force, or the accumulation of wealth from taxing his subjects.

"I must take a wife and she will bear me a son," he thought, "and that will surely fill this emptiness inside me." So he set about choosing a suitable bride. It couldn't be just any woman. It had to be a woman equal to the importance of the position — strong, wise, healthy, virtuous and above all beautiful.

The king sent messengers in six directions to look for her, with instructions to return in twice thirteen days, having located the appropriate candidate, for a prize of a bag of gold. The messengers set off on fast horses and the king went about his business of ruling and fighting and judging and imprisoning and taxing, and all the other jobs done by a warrior king who is largely indifferent to the welfare of his subjects.

A messenger returned in thirteen days and he was so breathless with excitement that he could hardly speak. "Her name is Solitaire and she is everything the you asked for and more," he said. "She is wise and strong and healthy and virtuous and very, very beautiful."

The warrior king was delighted and gladly gave the messenger his reward. He put on his best armour, saddled his very best horse and began his journey to his future wife. He arrived at Solitaire's door, accompanied by all his attendants and servants, with fanfare and pomp.

Solitaire greeted the king coolly, without much enthusiasm. She had always promised herself that she would marry for love and had no intention of going off with this arrogant man to live as his wife.

The warrior king got right down to business, saying, "I have come here to claim you as my wife. I have many fine lands and great wealth. You will bear me a son and he will take over my kingdom. You will be well treated and will live a life of ease and comfort. You will have servants and fine clothes."

Solitaire listened closely to his words and watched the expression on his face, and she knew that this man's heart was hard and that he would never love her the way she needed to be loved. However, she was also frightened of refusing him, for she had no doubt that a rejection would result in bad consequences for her.

An idea came to her. "I will marry you," she said, "if you bring me four gifts in four days, and if I find those gifts acceptable."

The warrior king agreed immediately, for he had brought with him the finest things from his land to offer to his bride-to-be. "I'll return with your first gift tomorrow." Of course, Solitaire had no intention of finding any of the gifts acceptable.

The warrior king returned the next day with a peach, golden and sweet. He handed it to Solitaire and as he did, her fingertips grazed his hand; it was cold and rough. She shivered inside and slowly turned the peach over and over in her hands, looking at it thoughtfully. She handed it back to the warrior king and said, looking him straight in the eye, "Thank you, but I would rather have a lemon. A peach you just eat and, although it is delicious, it is quickly gone." "A lemon," she said, "I can slice and use to season many fine dishes, then dry the peel to flavour the cider this winter."

The king was visibly annoyed at Solitaire's rude behaviour, but he was prepared to stick to his side of the bargain. Besides, Solitaire did not know about his dream cushion, so bringing her a lemon the next day would be easy. So he took the peach with him and promised to return the next day.

That night, he slept on his dream cushion and dreamed about the peach. And while he slept, the peach began to change. The stone in the centre became tiny pips, the delicate skin turned into hard rind, and the sweet taste became bitter.

The warrior king woke up to find that the peach had become a lemon and he smiled.

He went again to Solitaire's house with the lemon and a beautiful, tiny bird in a bamboo cage. Solitaire thanked the warrior king for the lemon and slipped it into her pocket. She was surprised that he had been able to find one so quickly but she did not let it show on her face.

The warrior king then gave her the bird and she held the cage up and looked inside at the small creature. Again, to the king's amazement, she handed it back to him. "Thank you. However, I would really rather have a cricket because they bring good luck and are not so noisy or difficult to care for."

The king left, cage in hand, and rode sullenly back to his lodgings. "I'm reaching the end of my patience," he thought. "But, it will be worth it when she is my wife and bears me a fine son."

That night, the king slept on his dream cushion and dreamed of the tiny bird. And while he slept, the bird began to change. Its feathers faded away and a hard skin appeared, its sharp beak became a blunt snout, and its tuneful singing changed to a high-pitched chirping.

The warrior king woke up to find that the bird had become a cricket and he smiled.

He set off for Solitaire's home with the cricket and thirteen red roses to offer her as her third gift. Solitaire greeted him politely and thanked him for the cricket. She was surprised that he had located one so quickly, because crickets were so difficult to catch. But, she calmly accepted the roses from him and looked at them carefully. She could smell their sweet perfume and feel the thorns pressing into her hands. She handed them back to a very surprised king and said, "Thank you. But, I'd really rather have some garlic. Roses are beautiful, but they fade and then you are left with nothing. Garlic keeps away colds, adds flavour to food and it lasts for months."

The king was furious as he left with the roses. He held them so hard, the thorns cut into his skin. He rode back to his lodgings, thinking, "She is the most ungrateful woman I have ever met in all my life!"

That night, the king slept on his dream cushion and dreamed of the roses. While he slept, their colour changed from bright red to milky white, the soft petals became firm cloves covered with a papery skin, and their sweet fragrance changed to a pungent aroma.

The warrior king awoke to find that the roses had changed to garlic and he smiled.

He started toward Solitaire's house with the garlic and a bolt of silk cloth. Solitaire accepted the garlic and cloth. She looked at the silk closely and ran her hand over the smooth, soft surface of the fabric. She handed the bolt of silk back to him and said, "Thank you, but I would rather have wool. Silk is beautiful but not very practical. Wool is sturdier and more versatile. Please bring me a bolt of wool."

This time, the king could not control himself any longer. "This is the finest silk in all the land! It cost a hundred gold pieces and one of my best horses!"

"Just the same," said Solitaire, "I would rather have wool."

So the angry king returned to his lodgings to try once again. "Never mind. It makes no difference," he said to himself, as he rode back home, "tonight I will dream of the silk, and its fine, shiny texture will become thicker and heavier. And, when I wake up, it will be a bolt of wool and then she will have to marry me."

That night, the frustrated warrior king fell asleep on his dream cushion. In his dream, he looked everywhere for the silk, but could not find it. He was in a hall of mirrors and all that he could see was himself. And so, while he slept, his hard heart began to soften. His cold hands began to warm and become sensitive again, his harsh voice became softer, his smile gradually widened and the muscles in his rigid face relaxed.

When the warrior king woke up the next morning, the bolt of silk was still a bolt of silk. He sat by the window to watch the sun rise and he smiled.

A Guided Visualisation: The Goddess Uli

SCRIPT FOR THE GUIDE: (To be read in a gentle trance-inducing voice.) Make yourself comfortable and close your eyes. Take a few deep breaths to help you relax. Feel the tension disappear stage by stage from the top of your head to the tips of your toes. Let your surroundings fade away as you gradually sink backwards through time and actuality and pass through the gateway of reality into the dreamtime. (When the participants are fully relaxed, begin the next stage.)

You're standing in a forest on a moonlit night and the trees are silhouetted against the silvery light. Open your inner eyes and see the forest around you. Hear the owls hooting and feel the whispering breeze that rustles the leaves in the trees. Now look for a path which leads deep into the forest and begin to walk along it – stepping over fallen tree-trunks, pushing low branches out of the way, and hearing the crunch of your steps on the leaves underfoot. Eventually you come to a grassy clearing, brightly lit by the moon, and you settle down in the centre and wait. You *have a minute of clock time, equal to all the time you need, to appreciate the scene....*

While you're sitting in the clearing, a swirling mist descends and out of it the goddess Uli appears, dressed in robes of deepest purple. Uli, the Polynesian goddess of magic, has the power to manifest dreams. "Tell me what your hopes are for the future and you will see them enacted." You have a minute of clock time, equal to all the time you need, to tell Uli your dreams and to see them brought to life in front of you....

"Now that you've danced your dreams awake in this enchanted forest, you can take them back with you to ordinary reality and dance them awake there too. You have the power to take control of your life and all you need is to have faith and to trust in the process." Uli then leads you to a waterfall where you can refresh yourself. You have a minute of clock time, equal to all the time you need, to let the cascading water cleanse you and wash all your doubts and uncertainties away....

The time has now come to thank the goddess for the help she has given you and to make your journey home – out of the grassy clearing and back along the pathway, crunching the fallen leaves underfoot, until you find yourself back where you started.

Open your eyes now and stretch your arms and legs. Welcome home! Take a few minutes in silence to make some notes on the experiences you had on your journeys, which you can then share with the rest of the group/make a note of in your dream journal.

– based on an idea from Gill Edwards, *Stepping Into The Magic*.

Making a Deathdoll is a Native American practice which helps you to let go of the old to allow the new in. The process entails making a doll to which you attach all your pain. As you find suitable objects to represent your concerns, you bring those objects to the pain in your body. The idea is to push your pain into the object, then attach it to the place on the doll that seems appropriate. When the doll is complete, it is ceremonially buried, leaving you free to start a new cycle. Then you can set about building your Lifedoll to represent the dreams you hope to dance awake. The Lifedoll is an object for you to keep and cherish as it represents your preferred scenario.

Deathdoll

I've made you many times before
And no doubt I'll make you again
For however often I bury you
Your return is inevitable

You rise to the surface from a hidden source
Seemingly inexhaustible
And what we are conscious of
Is merely the tip of the iceberg

Deathdoll
Let me nail my pain to you
Decorate you with my suffering
Mark you with my scars

Deathdoll
Let me transform you into my image
To purge myself of the growth that's eating me up
And sapping my life-force

Then let me give you a dignified burial
And leave you behind me
Ready for a new beginning
Having learnt from my experience.

Lifedoll

Lifedoll
Let me craft you with love
To rise out of the rut I've stuck myself in
My limited horizons, my blinkered vision

Let me decorate you with feathers
And weave you a pair of wings
So you can fly with my prayers to the upper World
And return with their manifestation

Lifedoll
Let me paint you all the colours of the rainbow
To lift me out of my black and white life
To be aware of the spectrum of possibilities that lie before me

Let me imbue you with my wildest dreams
And dance you awake to the beat of my drum
Let me hold you in my heart
And never lose sight of you

Lifedoll
May I always treasure you
And treat you with the reverence you deserve
So you can truly express my intent.

To the Sacred Site

[The Teachings of the Ancient Ones]

Stonehenge*

One piece of magic that never fails to cast a spell over the traveller is the awe-inspiring sight of Stonehenge appearing on the horizon as one crosses Salisbury Plain. There is nothing quite like this famous prehistoric monument anywhere else in the world.

Started five thousand years ago and remodelled several times in the following centuries, we can really apply only supposition and guess-work to interpret the reason for Stonehenge's existence. In more recent times a great many unlikely suggestions have been advanced as to the purpose and origin of the stones, ranging from Roman temple and druids to spaceship launch pads and ancient Greek architects. There is no proof for any of these, but one fact is certain: the major axis of Stonehenge was carefully aligned with the midwinter and midsummer sun. There are other alignments too, such as with the rising and setting of the moon, and all these point to Stonehenge being built for ceremonies to mark the annual calendar and seasons.

What amazing lengths the prehistoric builders went to in constructing such a monument! It is only for us to imagine how, with only primitive tools to help them, men cut and shaped these huge stones. Even more extraordinary, the massive stone lintels are mortice-and-tenoned to the uprights upon which they rest, and are curved to follow the circumference of the circle. Nor were they local stones – some were brought twenty miles from the Marlborough Downs, but the smaller Bluestones were brought from the Preseli Mountains in south-west Wales! Without machines or roads as we know them, it was a truly exceptional feat of organisation.

From afar, Stonehenge may seem disappointingly small, for we are used to being dwarfed by modern buildings. Close to, its grandeur is clear. Bearing in mind that some of the stones making up the outer ring and inner horseshoe of uprights with lintels weigh over fifty tons each. These are the hard, bare facts about this monument, which tell us what great things the earliest inhabitants of these islands could achieve – even if we remain unclear about their

* Some of the material in this section has been sourced from:
  www.fortunecity.com/roswell/blavatsky/123/stonebuilt.html

purpose. The mystery surrounding Stonehenge still seems as perpetual as the stones themselves.

Exercise for Teachers of English as a Foreign Language
When using the introductory text in class, you might prefer to present it as a cloze test.

One piece of magic that never (1) ... to cast a spell over the traveller is the awe-inspiring sight of Stonehenge appearing on the horizon as one crosses Salisbury Plain. (2) ... is nothing quite like this famous prehistoric monument (3) ... else in the world.

Started five thousand years ago and remodelled several times in the following centuries, we can really apply only supposition and guess-work to interpret the (4) ... for Stonehenge's existence. In more recent (5) ... a great (6) ... unlikely suggestions have been advanced as to the purpose and origin of the stones, ranging (7) ... Roman temple and druids to spaceship launch pads and ancient Greek architects. There is no (8) ... for any of these, but one fact is certain: the major axis of Stonehenge was carefully aligned with the midwinter and midsummer sun. There are other alignments too, (9) ... as with the rising and setting of the moon, and all these (10) ... to Stonehenge being built for ceremonies to mark the annual calendar and seasons.

What (11) ... lengths the prehistoric builders went to in constructing (12) ... a monument. It is (13) ... for us to imagine how, with only primitive (14) ... to help them, men cut and shaped these huge stones. Even (15) ... extraordinary, the massive stone lintels are mortice-and-tenoned to the uprights upon (16) ... they rest, and are curved to follow the circumference of the circle. Nor were they local stones – some were brought twenty miles from the

Marlborough Downs, but the smaller Bluestones were brought from the Preseli Mountains in south-west Wales! (17) ... machines or roads as we know them, it was a (18) ... exceptional feat of organisation.

(19) ... afar, Stonehenge may seem disappointingly small, for we are (20) ... to being dwarfed by modern buildings. Close to, its grandeur is clear. (21) ... in mind that some of the stones making up the outer ring and inner horseshoe of uprights with lintels (22) ... over fifty tons each. These are the hard, bare facts about this monument, (23) ... tell us what great things the earliest inhabitants of these islands could achieve – (24) ... if we remain unclear (25) ... their purpose. The mystery surrounding Stonehenge still seems as perpetual as the stones themselves.

ANSWERS: 1. fails 2. There 3. anywhere 4. reason 5. times 6. many 7. from 8. proof 9. such 10. point 11. amazing 12. such 13. only 14. tools 15. more 16. which 17. Without 18. truly 19. From 20. used 21. Bearing 22. weigh 23. which 24. even 25. about

---

Stonehenge can be found at the top of a gentle slope on the chalk downlands of Salisbury Plain, eight miles north of the town of Salisbury in southern England about eighty miles from London. It consists of 162 stones and is 35 paces across. These stones are menhirs, or big, tall, pillars protruding from the earth. Some are sandstone, and others are blue stone. The ruins of the magnificent circular stone structure stand inside a 320 foot (97 metre) henge, or bank and ditch arrangement. Scientists named the most recognisable structure, the outer ring of stones, the sarsen circle. Inside that circle is another circle, of bluestones, and then a sarsen horseshoe. The innermost structure is a horseshoe of bluestones. All of this is around the Altar Stone, a bluestone, towards the back of the bluestone horseshoe.

Most scientists agree on the modern theory that three tribes built Stonehenge at three separate times. The first peoples to work on the site were Neolithic agrarians, in approximately 3000 BC. Archaeologists named them the Windmill Hill people after one of their earthworks on Windmill Hill, a landmark nearby. The Windmill Hill people were a band of the local peoples, from whom the name comes, and Neolithic tribe members from Eastern England. The Neolithic tribe members brought along with them a reverence for circles and symmetry. Together, they were one of the first semi-nomadic hunting and gathering groups with an agricultural economy. The Windmill Hill peoples had collective burials in large stone-encased tombs, some of which are very near Stonehenge. They built large circular furrows, or hill-top enclosures, dug around a mound. Most of their burial mounds point east-west. They raised cattle, sheep, goats, pigs, dogs, grew wheat and mined flint.

The second peoples on the site invaded Salisbury Plain around 2000 BC. They were the Beaker People who came from Europe at the end of the Neolithic Period. Their name comes from one of their ancient traditions. They would bury beakers, or pottery drinking cups, with their dead. They did not bury their dead in mass graves, but showed more reverence for death, also a sign of cultural advancement. They buried their dead in small round graves marked by mounds called tumuli. The Beaker People were probably more belligerent, or warlike in nature, than most tribes of their time because they buried their dead with more weapons, such as daggers and battleaxes. Scientists believe they were sun worshippers who aligned Stonehenge more exactly with certain important sun events, such as midsummer and winter solstices. They might have worshipped the colour blue, possibly the reason they used bluestones. They were highly organised, skilled in many crafts, and able to work with sophisticated mathematical concepts.

The third and final peoples at the Stonehenge site are the Wessex Peoples, who arrived around 1500 BC at the height of the Bronze Age. These people were one of the most advanced cultures outside the Mediterranean during this period. Since they located themselves where ridgeways, or ancient roads, met, they became skillful and well-organised traders, controlling trade routes throughout Southern Britain. Though this tribe saw great wealth, it was concentrated in just a few members of the society. It is possible that they were responsible for the bronze dagger carving recently found on one of the large sarsen stones. The strange thing about these peoples is their intelligence. They were capable of greater precision in their calculations and construction than these ancient peoples were first credited.

The name Stonehenge came from the Saxons. Originally, they called it Stanhenge. Stan is Old English for stone, and henge means 'to hang'. It is possible that the stones seemed to hang in the air, or those ancient peoples were reminded of medieval gallows. Some theorists speculate that people used Stonehenge to hang criminals, hence the name. However, we will never know for certain how the name was formed.

There are many myths and legends about Stonehenge. In the past, people have attributed the building of this great megalith to the Danes, Romans, Celts, Saxons, Greeks, Atlanteans, Egyptians, Phoenicians, and even King Aureoles Ambrosias and Merlin. In one legend, dancing giants turned into stone, resulting in the circular position of the stones. Some people today connect Stonehenge with UFOs and aliens, pointing out that crop circles and ley lines continually appear in close vicinity to it.

Many past archaeologists believed that the Druids, the high priests of the Celts, constructed it for sacrificial ceremonies. They believed that only such a mysterious and mystical group such as the Druids could build an ancient temple so magnificent as Stonehenge. In recent years, however, this age-old theory has been proven impossible. Due to modern dating techniques, scientists have discovered that its builders completed Stonehenge over 1,000 years before the Celts ever inhabited this region, eliminating them from the possibilities. It is true, although, that the Druids did use Stonehenge occasionally as a temple of worship and sacrifice when they moved into the region, even though they typically worshipped in marshes and forests. Modern Druids, formally named the Grand Lodge of the Ancient Order of Druids, still congregate at Stonehenge on the midsummer solstice, clad in white robes and hoods.

A number of sources cite the devil, nonetheless, as a possible architect of Stonehenge. It is said that an old woman living in Ireland had the stones in her backyard. Satan discovered them and wanted them for his own. He quickly devised a way of stealing them. Dressing as a gentleman, the devil is said to have visited the old lady, asking if the monument was for sale. When she appeared reluctant to sell such a magnificent structure, he showed her a large bag of golden coins. He told her that she could have all the gold she could count in the time it took to move the stones. Believing that he could never move such large stones before she finished counting the coins, she agreed readily. Immediately he magically transported them to Salisbury Plain in England, where they stand today. The old lady could not count any gold in that short amount of time, so the greedy devil kept it all. Back in Salisbury, an elderly priest overheard the devil bragging that no one would ever be able to tell how many stones his prize consisted of. Angered by the devil's boasting, the wise and strong priest said that he could. According to legend, he guessed exactly right. The devil became so enraged that he threw one of the large stones at the priest and it hit him on his heel. However, the priest was so strong that his heel dented the stone. Obviously, this tale is purely myth. But oddly enough, there is the imprint of a foot in the stone that archaeologists today call the Heel stone, and it stands outside the circle.

Another legend boasts that Merlin built Stonehenge with his magic at the command of King Aureoles Ambrosias. According to legend, in AD 450, there was a very bloody war on Salisbury Plain between the British and the Saxons. The Saxons massacred three hundred English soldiers and buried them on Salisbury Plain. Aureoles Ambrosias, Britain's wise ruler, desired a monument to the slain soldiers. When he asked Merlin for ideas, he suggested moving Ireland's Giant's Ring stone circle to Britain. Since the Giant's Ring was such a magnificent structure, King Ambrosias agreed. When arriving in Ireland, they discovered that it was much larger than they could carry. So, at King Ambrosias' command, Merlin magically dismantled the stone circle and spirited it away to its new home in Salisbury Plain, around the mass grave of the slaughtered noblemen. It is also said that Kings Uther, Constantine, and King Ambrosias himself are buried there.

The real purpose of Stonehenge may never be known and all we can do is to make educated guesses and inferences from what little the builders left behind. The current and most popular belief is that it was an advanced calendar to mark, to predict and to observe astronomical and seasonal events such as summer and winter solstice, equinox and lunar eclipses. It is quite possible that, in its first stage, Stonehenge was purely a religious structure, and modified by later builders to serve as an astronomical observatory.

Stonehenge these days is a major sightseeing attraction and is visited by coachloads of tourists. To protect the site from vandals, the stones are now surrounded by railings and much of the magic of the place has been lost. For an impression of Stonehenge in all its former glory, it is recommended that you visit the site outside public opening hours. Alternatively, you might like to explore some of the other ancient stone circles, less accessible to and less frequented by tourists.

Stonehenge is a well-known site visited by thousands of tourists. However, there are many other circles to be found in England, for example the Rollright Stones in Oxfordshire. Nobody really knows for sure what the circle was originally used for but here's a folk tale that offers a possible explanation.

The Rollright Stones

At the head of his dwindling army, the king strode on. What his name was, or where he came from, there is now no chance of knowing; but that he was on foot, and that his intention was to subdue the rest of England, is tradition that must not be questioned.

The way had been long, and the travelling hard. Of those who had set out with the king, many had regretted their allegiance, and had sneaked off in the darkness towards their homes again. Younger men had deserted along the route, tempted by the warmth and comfort of a cottage hearthstone, or the lure of a pair of rounded thighs. Still more had fallen out, sick or wounded from skirmishes among themselves as well as among the unwelcoming inhabitants of the lands they had passed through. Now they were reduced to three score and ten, or thereabouts, seventy-two or seventy-three, or even only seventy-one; the king could not be sure.

Among them, though, were their five captains, the lords at whose command they had first left the comfort of their homes to follow the king. As close as brothers were these five, forever finding excuses for putting their heads together and whispering words not meant for the king to hear. He was well aware of their intrigue, but kept himself aloof, sure of his own power and of his own judgment, and confident of success in his purpose. Over the next line of hills lay a stretch of countryside vital to his overall conquest. So up the slope he plodded, while the five knights stayed close together, a little distance away.

When he was nearly at the top, a figure appeared on the brow, facing him as he strode on. It was the figure of an aged woman, gnarled and twisted but with a commanding presence. She held up her hand in a gesture that stopped him in his tracks and all his followers with him.

"What do you want?" she asked, in a voice of chilling power.

"Passage across the hill. No one stands in my way."

"The hill is mine, and the land all round it," she replied. "What is your purpose?"

"To conquer England, and rule it as one kingdom."

She gave a cackle of mocking laughter, holding out a long finger with which she pointed to the brow of the hill.

"Ah, so I thought," she said.

"Seven strides more is my prophecy,
And if Long Compton you can see,
King of England you shall be!"

The king measured with his eye the distance to the top of the slope, and saw indeed that it was about seven paces. He was now within a few yards of succeeding in his enterprise, if only the old crone could be believed, and he had no reason to doubt her prophecy. So he turned to face his army, and cried out in exultation,

"Stick, stock and stone,
As King of England I shall be known!"

Then he turned about again, and began to pace out his seven long strides towards the top of the hill; but to his great chagrin, there rose before him a long mound of earth that completely obscured the view down into the valley. And there he stood, while his five knights drew close together whispering to each other, and his men spread out in a loose semi-circle behind him.

Then the witch raised her arm again, and in a loud voice cried,

"Because Long Compton you cannot see,
King of England you shall not be.
Rise up stick, and stand still stone,
King of England you shall not become.
You and your men solid stone shall be,
And I myself an elder tree!"

Then the king (and every man with him) felt his feet turn cold as stone, and so heavy on the earth that strength could not raise them an inch; and gradually the freezing numbness crept upwards, till king, knights and men all had been turned to solid blocks of stone.

And there they are to this day, at Little Rollright in the Cotswolds – the Kingstone tall and commanding, a little apart as a king should be; the five knights with their heads together, plotting still, and the men scattered around and about them in a loose, wide circle. Ask not how many men there are, for though the number is thought to be seventy-two, no one is ever able to count them and make the number the same on two successive counts.

There are those who believe that the king still waits, like Arthur and King Redbeard, for the curse to be lifted, when he will march forward again with his men to confound his enemies and take over the realm of England. In the meantime, as he waits while age upon age rolls past, he is surrounded by elder trees, progeny of that tree into which the old crone magicked herself upon that fateful day. It is best not to visit the Rollright Stones on Midsummer Eve, for then, they say, if you stick a knife into one of the elder trees, it will not be sap that runs, but blood; and at the sight of it, the stone that was once a king will bend and bow his head, acknowledging still its power.

The five knights still whisper their treachery to each other as the evening breeze drifts round them; but though many have set out in the moonlight to eavesdrop on their whispering, no one yet has ever stayed long enough to hear what they have to say.

No doubt it is better that way.

Sacred places, like the painted caves at Lascaux in South-western France or historic cathedrals throughout Europe, foster experiences reminiscent of a holding environment. In such spaces we are reminded of the promise of connection and the value of purpose in our lives. Some such sacred places are remote or inaccessible enough for us to be able to hold ceremonies there without being disturbed. Alternatively, we can find them in other realities through journeying.

A Guided Visualisation: To The Sacred Site

SCRIPT FOR THE GUIDE: (To be read in a gentle trance-inducing voice.) Make yourself comfortable and close your eyes. Take a few deep breaths to help you relax. Feel the tension disappear stage by stage from the top of your head to the tips of your toes. Let your surroundings fade away as you gradually sink backwards through time and actuality and pass through the gateway of reality into the dreamtime. (When the participants are fully relaxed, begin the next stage.)

Now travel back to a time long ago, back to a time long before so-called 'civilisation', back to a time when we still knew how to live in harmony with Nature, back to a time when we still knew how to use all the powers we are born with.

It's night and you're standing at the foot of a hill with a canopy of stars overhead. You see a procession of hooded figures in long flowing robes climbing up the hillside. You take your place in the line and follow behind them. Like the others, you walk in silence, carrying a torch to light the way, and you sense the importance of the occasion. The wind's blowing strongly against you, which makes the climb difficult, but like everyone else you're determined to reach the top because you sense something special awaits you. Eventually you reach the crest of the hill and you're not disappointed – because there bathed in moonlight is the ceremonial site, the sacred place to which you've been called. You have a minute of clock time, equal to all the time you need, to reflect on what you can see there....

You form a circle around the site with all the other hooded figures and wait for the ceremony to start. Standing in the centre, you see a figure dressed in white and this person seems to be beckoning to you. At first you think someone else is being summoned, not you, because surely you're not important enough to receive such an honour. However, it soon becomes clear that it's you being called so you walk towards the figure. You have a minute of clock time, equal to all the time you need, to study the Sacred Teacher standing in front of you....

The figure dressed in white addresses you. "You're here for a very important reason. Listen carefully to what I have to say because it will help you on your future journey through life. You have no need to ask any questions because I can read your mind and I know you better than you know yourself. All you have to do is listen." You have a minute of clock time, equal to all the time you need, to listen to the words of your Sacred Teacher....

Now you hear the call-back sound, the sound of a horn, and you know that it's time to return again. Thank your Teacher for the help you've been given and make your way back, the same way you came, down the side of the hill and forward through time, back to the place where you started.

Open your eyes now and stretch your arms and legs. Welcome Home! Take a few minutes in silence to make some notes on the experiences you had on your journeys, which you can then share with the rest of the group/make a note of in your dream journal.

Conflict & Resolution

[Be like the Wind ... Let Conflict Blow Through You]

On a journey to the Upper World to deal with a problem I was having, I was told to be like the wind and to let conflict blow through me – but easier said than done! I'm also reminded of a postcard I picked up in a New Age shop once, saying that we shouldn't judge another person until we'd walked a certain number of miles in their moccasins. If we can only remember that we're all part of the same Great Mystery, and that if we hurt another person we are hurting only ourselves, then the motivation to resolve disputes becomes all pervasive. The Origin Of Strawberries is a simple but moving Native American tale, the Polynesian Goddess of beauty Hina is the source of inspiration for the visualisation, and Christmas Peace is a present day parable to help us to remove discord from our lives.

The Origin of Strawberries

When the world was still young, there was a man and a woman. Sometimes they were happy, sometimes they quarrelled. One day the woman left her husband and went east, to the land of the Sun. The husband followed her. He asked her to forgive him, but the wife continued to walk and did not look back.

The Sun felt sorry for the husband and said, "Are you still angry with your wife?"

The man said, "No!"

The Sun said, "Do you want her back?"

"Yes," said the man.

So the Sun let some huckleberries grow at the feet of the woman. The woman passed by, without taking any notice of the huckleberries. Then the Sun planted blackberry bushes on the way, but the woman went past them too. Next the Sun put blueberries along the woman's path, but still she continued walking away.

Again and again the Sun tried to tempt the woman with different types of berry and fruit but still the woman did not look back.

Then the Sun created a bed of delicious ripe strawberries. They were the first strawberries. And when the woman saw them, she stopped. To pick some of the strawberries, she had to turn to face the west. When she did this, she had to think of her husband. She wanted to turn again towards the Land of the Sun but she could not go any further. *She could not go any further.*

Then the woman picked some strawberries and ate them. She turned her back on the Land of the Sun and saw her husband. They both went back to their tent together.

A Guided Visualisation: The Goddess Hina

SCRIPT FOR THE GUIDE: *(To be read in a gentle trance-inducing voice.) Make yourself comfortable and close your eyes. Take a few deep breaths to help you relax. Feel the tension disappear stage by stage from the top of your head to the tips of your toes. Let your surroundings fade away as you gradually sink backwards through time and actuality and pass through the gateway of reality into the dreamtime. (When the participants are fully relaxed, begin the next stage.)*

You're standing in front of the mouth of a cave and you stoop down low to enter it. You crawl along a tunnel that goes down into the earth until you come to a cavern with a cobblestoned floor that leads out into the sea.

The full moon illuminates a pathway across the water and you swim out to an island that lies on the other side. There on the beach to greet you is the goddess Hina. Hina is the Polynesian goddess of beauty with the power to help us live in harmony. You find her dressed in a long skin-tight dress of shimmering silver, with jet-black hair down to her waist. You tell Hina about a conflict you have with someone you know and ask her for guidance. You have a minute of clock time, equal to all the time you need, to tell her about your problem and to listen to what she has to say....

Hina says that she has a special gift for you which will help you to deal with your conflict. You have a minute of clock time, equal to all the time you need, to unwrap and appreciate your gift....

You thank the goddess for all the help she has given you and promise to act on the advice you've been given because you know you can trust her. Now the time has come to make your journey home, back across the sea to the mouth of the cobblestoned cavern, up through the narrow tunnel and back to the entrance of the cave, out into the open air again.

Open your eyes now and stretch your arms and legs. Welcome home! Take a few minutes in silence to make some notes on the experiences you had on your journeys, which you can then share with the rest of the group/make a note of in your dream journal.

Christmas Peace

It was late on Christmas Eve at the old people's home. Bill was alone in his room, drinking sherry. He had been a soldier as a young man in the second world war and had seen service in Africa in the army. There was an old black-and-white photo of him in uniform on the wall by his bed.

Had the war been worth it? The loss of life on both sides, the injuries, the hell of it all? Perhaps war was inevitable. Perhaps the cynics were right when they said that peace was just an interlude between wars. Bill had once believed in the possibility of a world at peace and harmony but now he was not so sure. Was peace possible, even desirable?

"Have faith, Bill," a voice said inside his head. A great feeling of peace filled him and Bill listened intently for the voice to come again, but there was only silence.

After some moments he heard the voice again.

"Listen Bill," it said. "Peace is real. Can't you feel it?" Bill sat upright in his armchair. Yes. His pains and fears and negativities had subsided. He felt good. A smile came to his face.

The voice continued. "Be still and enjoy the peace within you. There is great strength in peace. There is great comfort in peace. The greatest service you can give your fellow man is to share your peace with him."

"But how can I maintain this peace?" Bill wondered to himself. "There are so many problems and annoyances in everyday life."

"But are any of those problems and irritations worth the price of giving up your peace?" asked the voice.

Bill sat back just enjoying the profound stillness and sense of well-being that filled him. "If only I could feel like this always," he thought.

"You can." said the voice, "You can."

Bill believed it. This feeling of peace was so completely satisfying. He could see that if all people were in this state, there could be no enmity between individuals or wars between nations.

"So what can I do for peace?" he wondered.

"You can take away others' pain," the voice replied.

"What does that mean?" asked Bill.

"Just watch and listen," came the answer. "Go into the lounge and leave everything to me."

Bill got up and went into the lounge of the home. The lounge was bedecked with Christmas decorations and there was a tree with coloured lights in the far corner. Two blue-uniformed care assistants were in attendance and about a dozen of the residents sat about in chairs, dozing or watching a film on TV.

"Hello, Bill," said Gloria, the older of the assistants. "How are you this evening?" she asked.

"Fine, thank you," Bill answered with a smile. She looked at him surprised. Bill rarely said he was fine and never smiled.

"How are you, Gloria?" Bill asked.

"Fine, thank you," she answered.

He beamed at her. "I hope you have a great Christmas," he said.

"And how are you this evening, Sarah?" Bill asked the younger of the assistants, an attractive dark-haired woman in her late twenties.

"All right, thanks," she replied a little coldly. Bill smiled warmly at her and wished her a happy Christmas too.

Bill looked around at all the residents in their armchairs and transmitted a feeling of affection to each of them in turn. He couldn't remember having felt so good. Silently he wished them all, even the grumpy ones, "Happy Christmas" from the bottom of his heart.

"Go back to your room now," said the voice in his head. With one last look around him, Bill walked out of the lounge.

"Has Bill been on the sherry?" Sarah asked Gloria when Bill had left.

"I don't know," answered Gloria. "Perhaps he's caught some of the Christmas spirit!"

Bill sat down in the chair in his room again.

"Well, do you see what you can do for peace?"

"What do you mean?" asked Bill.

"Can't you see that when you extend to others the peace within you that you can take away their pain?"

"Did I do that in the lounge?" asked Bill.

"Yes, you did. Just a little, but yes, you did."

Bill looked at the Christmas cards on his table. They included one from his son, John. Bill hadn't sent John a card because they had had a row some weeks ago. With tears in his eyes, he took out a blank card and wrote: To John, with love from Dad.

"It's not too late to send this, is it?" he asked himself.

"No," came the answer. "It's never too late."

The clock struck twelve. Christmas had arrived.

Moving On
[Leaving the Past Behind You]

The time has come to leave the past behind, to put the lessons learnt in non-ordinary reality into practice and to dance the dreams awake. The parable of *The Snooker Hall Ghost* is the starting point, a journey through awakening to finding inner peace and then no turning back. There will undoubtedly be further challenges on the road ahead, but in the visualisation the Mebodishe contacts the batonebi, the spirits sent to test us, to negotiate with them on our behalf. This ending is no more than a beginning so let go of the old ways that no longer serve you to allow the new to take hold. As Joseph Campbell said, "We must be willing to get rid of the life we've planned so as to have the life that is waiting for us".

The Snooker Hall Ghost

Snooker has always been my game. I suppose that's why I'm a snooker hall ghost now that I'm dead. It's not a year-round job. I work in a holiday camp in the north of England, May to September, and then back to the celestial realms from October to April.

I don't do much when I'm at work, just drift around the room, trying to give a bit of encouragement here and a bit of advice there. Of course, I'm invisible to all the players but often I can get something through. It's not a bad job as ghosts' jobs go. At least most of the people in the hall are enjoying themselves.

My story begins nearly five months ago, near the start of the season, during a wet Monday in late May when the hall was really crowded: all fifteen tables were in use. I had noticed the young man as soon as he entered the room. His physical appearance was unremarkable: five foot ten, dark hair, slim, but he had a beautiful golden aura around him, not a full shining aura but definitely a golden aura. I had never seen such an aura around anybody in the snooker hall before.

He was with his girlfriend, teaching her to play it seemed. I drifted over to their table to watch them. Then, during the slow progress through the reds, he looked at me, right into my eyes. It gave us both a shock. He stopped playing and continued staring at me.

"What's up? What are you looking at?" the girl asked.

"I don't know," he answered. "I can't be sure. I thought I saw someone standing at the end of the table, looking at us."

"Don't be daft," she said, looking at the empty space beyond the table where I was standing. "Get on with the game."

A few minutes later, the reds had been cleared and he was now ready to take on the colours. The yellow was sitting nicely near a corner pocket, about three feet from the white. It was an easy shot, needing just a little bit of side.

"Yellow, the colour of awakening," I thought.

"The colour of awakening?" I heard him think. Had he heard my thought? This was most unusual!

"Yes," I replied. "Pot the yellow."

"Go in, you yellow," he said, lining up the shot and thrusting the cue smartly forwards, striking the white ball. It travelled firmly into the yellow, which went directly into the jaws of the top right corner pocket.

"Good shot, John," his girlfriend shouted.

"Yellow, the colour of awakening, John," I said.

John sat down on a chair by the side of the table. His eyes were open in wonder, his expression a mixture of sadness and joy.

"Are you all right?" his girlfriend asked.

"Yes, I feel just a little bit faint," he replied.

I smiled at him. I knew he could see me and hear me, and I knew exactly what he was feeling at this moment.

"Well potted," I said. "It feels good to be awake, doesn't it?" John nodded and smiled.

"See you tomorrow?" I asked. "You could go for the brown tomorrow."

I could hear his thought in reply: "See you tomorrow," it said. Then John asked, "What does the brown ball stand for?"

"Brown, John, is the colour of peace." I answered.

John's experience of awakening brought back my own experience of so many years ago. I took the rest of the day off. I knew the Boss wouldn't mind. I drifted over to the lake and just sat and watched the water and the sky and the birds, and I marvelled. Finally, I had made a real difference. I had helped a human being to awaken. I sat staring at the lake. I had to give it to the Boss; he had created such a beautiful world.

John didn't come the next day or the day after that. I wasn't surprised. Awakening was such a profound experience that many people were happy not to move on for months, even years.

Thursday morning he didn't come either. I wanted to look for him to ask him to come but I knew that was against the rules. Thursday evening, just as I was sure he wouldn't come, the door opened and there he was. John was by himself this time. He looked round the room until he saw me. Then, he found an empty table, put the brown ball on its spot and positioned the white a foot behind it and to the left to give him an angle to the right-hand middle pocket.

"Right," he said, "I'm ready. The colour of peace you say. Let's see."

I watched as he hit the white hard against the brown. The brown hit the cushion just to the right of the pocket and bounced back. John had missed! He looked at me, aghast.

"Take the shot again," I said calmly.

"Can I?" he asked, astonished.

"Why not?" I replied, "It's only a stupid game." I couldn't believe I had said that. Snooker had been my whole life. I had been a national junior champion and a middling professional.

John set the shot up again and I gave him some advice about his shot. He hit the ball carefully and deliberately. This time the brown ball went straight into the pocket.

"My God," he said quietly as soon as the ball had dropped. "It's happening already."

"Take your time," I said. "Enjoy the experience. You will never know fear again."

"I believe you," he answered, "But how does it work? People pot snooker balls all the time, but these experiences don't happen to everybody every day, do they?"

"Look, John. I'm not a philosopher or a priest. I'm just a snooker hall ghost. I don't know how it works either. All I can tell you is that these experiences or initiations happen to everybody sooner or later, in one lifetime or another. You will help somebody to experience one or other of these steps one day. This week, it's my turn to help you."

"I see," said John. "So, are you saying that there are initiations for the other four colours as well?"

"Yes, there are, and others beyond those."

"So, are you going to help me with the green, blue, pink and black balls too?"

"No, John, I'm sorry," I answered him. "I can't do that. The green ball is as far as I go. I haven't reached blue yet."

"Well, how will you reach blue then?" John asked.

"I don't know," I answered. "When the time is right I suppose."

"And what about green for me?" he asked.

"That's up to you. When does your holiday finish? Saturday?"

He nodded.

"Well, that leaves tomorrow. I'll be here all day."

"Why don't I do it now?" he asked.

"... OK," I said, taken aback. But – why not? "Set the green up. Do it!"

"What does the green stand for?" John asked as he put the green on its spot.

"It means no going back. It means saying yes to whatever your mission is in life and not taking refuge in lies or shadows. Do you still want to go ahead with the shot?"

"I do," he replied without hesitation.

"Very well. Place the white wherever you want. Then, pot that green. You won't regret it, I promise you."

I watched in awe as John lined up the shot and pushed the cue forwards. It was a beautiful shot, firm and true. The green didn't touch the jaws of the pocket as it went diving down into the gloom of the net bag.

"Welcome to the green brotherhood, John," I said. "A lot of people choose to rest after the second initiation for years or lifetimes. You moved on in two minutes!"

"What about the blue?" John asked, his eyes shining.

"I'm sorry. I can't do that for you. If you pot the blue now, it won't mean anything. I haven't got the power to open that door for you even if you are ready for it. I'm sorry."

"Then why don't you pot the blue then?" he asked. "Perhaps it'll work for you?"

The idea seemed preposterous but I decided to give it a try. I put the blue on its spot and placed the white a short distance away. I chalked the cue, sized up the shot, and aimed for my favourite pocket, the top left-hand corner.

"You can do it," said John.

I hit the white ball gently. Slowly, it rolled across the green baize, and made contact with the blue ball which in its turn set sail across the sea of green towards the harbour entrance of the top left pocket. I held my breath, half hoping that it would miss. Life as the snooker hall ghost was not bad, and I knew things would not be the same if that ball went in. I waited as the blue completed its journey and unerringly went down that hole.

Suddenly, I was no longer in the hall. I didn't know where I was. I didn't know what was happening to me. Tremendous energies seemed to be pouring into me. And then, after goodness knows how long, I was back in the hall, standing next to the snooker table with John standing opposite me, looking perplexed.

"You disappeared," he said. "Where did you go?"

"I don't know," I answered. "I've no idea."

"What does it mean, the blue initiation?" he asked.

"I don't know, honestly," I replied. "But what I do know is that this will be my last season as the snooker hall ghost. In fact, I'm pretty sure my ghosting days are over. I think that you were why I was doing this job, so I'm through."

"But what about the blue initiation. Can you give that to me?" he asked. "I can set the table up now."

"No, John," I said as kindly as I could. "What I do understand now about the blue initiation is that you have to give the first three initiations to someone else before you can receive the blue initiation yourself."

"But how will I know who and when and how?" John asked.

"You will know just as I did. Now you must go. Goodbye and thank you."

John walked out of the door of the snooker hall, and I haven't seen him since. It is now nearly the end of September and there haven't been any more initiations or dramatic events this summer.

I was right though about my days as a ghost being over. I've been selected for training at the Angel Academy next month. I just hope they've got a snooker table there!

A Guided Visualisation: The Mebodishe

SCRIPT FOR THE GUIDE: (To be read in a gentle trance-inducing voice.) Make yourself comfortable and close your eyes. Take a few deep breaths to help you relax. Feel the tension disappear stage by stage from the top of your head to the tips of your toes. Let your surroundings fade away as you gradually sink backwards through time and actuality and pass through the gateway of reality into the dreamtime. (When the participants are fully relaxed, begin the next stage.)

Why should some people be rich while others are poor, and why should some people be healthy while others suffer from illness? None of us can know the answers to such questions but perhaps the batonebi have a part to play. The batonebi are the spirits sent among the people to test them, the spirits who reside in the bodies of the stricken. You're invited to take a minute of clock time, equal to all the time you need, to think of someone you know, perhaps a relative or a friend, who is having more than their fair share of bad luck, someone who could benefit from some assistance....

And now you have the opportunity to go on a special journey, a journey to meet with a mebodishe – a woman with the power to contact the batonebi and to win over their hearts. The mebodishe is an old woman who lives on her own, on a hillside on the outskirts of Tbilisi in the Republic of Georgia. She frightens people because she has no need of their help but you know that's what gives the mebodishe her power. You knock three times on the door of her house and the old lady welcomes you in. Despite her physical frailty, you can sense the power that flows through her and you know without any doubt that you've come to the right place. Take a minute of clock time, equal to all the time you need, to tell the mebodishe about your friend or relative and to ask her for her help....

"Ask yourself what you would be prepared to give up to help the person you've chosen," the mebodishe says. "What can I offer the batonebi to persuade them to leave your friend in peace?" Take a minute of clock time, equal to all the time you need, to answer the mebodishe's question and to tell her about the sacrifice you're prepared to make....

"I know that your intentions are good and I'll do everything I can to help you. I'll travel beyond the Black Sea to meet with the batonebi and to present your case. Know that whatever happens will be for the best and trust in the process. And now you must leave me to proceed with my work." You thank the mebodishe for her help you and say your goodbyes for it's time to make your journey home again.

And as you travel back from the mebodishe's house on the hill to the centre of the city, you remember the sacrifice you agreed to make and resolve to give what you can to help people less fortunate than yourself in future. So back you travel, through time and actuality, back, back, the same way you came, back through the gateway between the two worlds and back to the place you started from.

Open your eyes now and stretch your arms and legs. Welcome home! Take a few minutes in silence to make some notes on the experiences you had on your journey, which you can then share with the rest of the group/make a note of in your dream journal.

The Give-Away

One of the most important ceremonies in Native American teachings is the Give-Away. In this ceremony, giving away of useful or loved possessions is a form of sharing with others. It is also a sign that the giver is willing to make a sacrifice and surrender a gift to another person without attachment or regret. To make any act or any gift sacred, one has to complete that action with a joyful heart and a humble attitude. Giving is only one step of the process and allows the giver to look within so that he or she may examine the growth potential associated with the Give-Away. The magic of the Give-Away is that the more you release, the more you receive. It's all about relief through release, not getting stuck holding on to anything that no longer serves you. The Native Americans say that if you give away something that's important to you, then your life is renewed. It means that you have the things instead of the things having you. And if you can't give away your possessions, they will destroy you.

A Guided Visualisation: Moving On

SCRIPT FOR THE GUIDE: (To be read in a gentle trance-inducing voice.) Make yourself comfortable and close your eyes. Take a few deep breaths to help your relax. Feel the tension disappear stage by stage from the top of your head to the tips of your toes. Let your surroundings fade away as you gradually sink backwards through time and actuality and pass through the gateway of reality into the dreamtime. (When the participants are fully relaxed, begin the next stage.)

Picture yourself on the first day you started this programme, uncertain about your ability and unsure of yourself. Feel how you've grown in confidence and how the first day is now a distant memory. Look at the person you've become and how you've been transformed as a result of your experiences. You have a minute of clock time, equal to all the time you need, to enjoy and appreciate the positive changes that have taken place....

Now the time has come to leave this behind you, secure in the knowledge you no longer need such support, secure in the knowledge you can now manage your life on your own and that what you've learnt along the way will be retained. You have a minute of clock time, equal to all the time you need, to plant these thoughts firmly inside you to ensure they stay with you and to congratulate yourself on your achievements....

You are responsible for the progress you've made and nobody else. You're now in a position to take control of your life and there's no longer any need for you to regard yourself as a victim of circumstance. You've successfully dealt with your doubts and uncertainties in the dreamtime so it will be that much easier to cope in the realtime. You have all the equipment you need at your disposal and nothing to fear.

And now as I count slowly to ten, you'll return through the gateway you stepped through, back to reality, feeling refreshed and revitalised and ready for the next stage of your journey, with full confidence in your abilities. 1 – 2 – 3 – 4 – 5 – 6 – 7 – 8 – 9 – 10 – and welcome to your new life!

Open your eyes now and stretch your arms and legs. Take a few minutes in silence to make some notes on the experiences you had on your journey which you can then share with the rest of the group/make a note of in your dream journal.

The Closing Ceremony

I give thanks to the powers of the six directions
For honouring me with their presence
For aiding me to accomplish my task
For helping me to find my inner voice

And I give thanks to all my relations
And pray to feel every second
Of every minute, of every day
A sense of connection to you
For if I cause you damage in any way
Then I damage myself
As together we are all part of the same totality
And I pray that I never forget this.

The Epilogue: God's Story

Long, long ago, I was alone, terribly alone. No space, no time, no here and now. Just me. I was cosmically bored, infinitely lonely.

And so I decided to play a game, to construct a universe out of my imagination. First I created a huge number of energy centres that you call stars and then masses of rocks that you call planets. I set in motion huge forces and before my eyes the universe was created, a massive interacting system of energy fields governed by expansion and contraction, attraction and repulsion, stasis and movement.

Next, on some of the planets I put life, primitive life, and then I waited for what you would describe as aeons. I watched as the climates and the life on these planets evolved and changed. It was all so gloriously unpredictable, so fantastically exciting.

Slowly, the life forms became more and more conscious and then more and more questioning. The spirit of enquiry was born in the life forms of many of the solar systems, and then literature and science and engineering followed. I marvelled at all these developments: creatures struggling to understand who they were and why they existed.

Some of them even wondered who had created them and developed stories and myths about their creation. I was called Father or Mother or the Ultimate Cause. I yearned to communicate with these creatures, to know myself through them.

In a curious way, not only was I their creator, but in some senses they were my creator too: their developing comprehension of themselves and the universe mirrored my own. The diversity and complexity of my creatures amazed me.

But yet I was still sad. All of this creation and all of the millennia, and still I didn't understand myself. I still felt lonely and bewildered. What hope was there for me?

I began to wonder whether my experiment of creating the universe had been worthwhile after all. Perhaps I had created the universe in vain. I was thinking of closing down the whole system and going to sleep. Who would comfort me? Who would stop my pain?

"I will comfort you. I will stop your pain," said a voice. Who had spoken? I looked down and saw on the planet earth a young human female who was speaking to me.

"Can you hear my thoughts?" I asked.

"Yes, I can," she answered.

"How can you comfort me?" I asked. "I am God and you are just a young human."

"God, I have learnt compassion," she said.

"Tell me about this compassion," I said to her.

"My parents died when I was very small," she said. "I went to live with my grandmother," she said. "My grief was too much to bear, and then my grandmother was grieving too for the loss of her daughter, my mother. It was too much for me. In the end, the only way for me to deal with the pain was to give all the love I could to my grandmother. Finally, my heart broke and after that I felt nothing but love for all creatures. God, if you want to find peace, you too must break your heart in compassion for all your creatures."

I listened to the girl and I knew that she spoke the truth. What she said touched me in a way that nothing else had ever done.

I followed her advice and tried to love my creatures with all my might, and as she said, finally, my heart broke. I felt such love for all the creatures that I had created in their struggle for understanding and completion. How could I help them? After all, I had created them. I was responsible for them. Surely I could help them somehow.

How could I help to heal their pain? I sent teachers to give them the message of peace and love. I caused great religions to be formed and holy books to be created. And yet there was still pain and misunderstanding. What more could I do? And then I realised that the most potent agent for healing was the power of story telling. There had always been and would always be storytellers. The healing might be short-lived but it was a hope. At last, I felt glad. Religions would come and go but there would always be stories. If there were stories, there would be hope. I am a patient God, and I put my trust in the storytellers. Where there is the healing power of stories, there is hope. Where there is hope, there is joy.

Appendix One

Exercises for Young Learners

Our parents spend all their lives looking after us. What do we do to help them? That's what this story from China is all about.

The Young Man and the Ice

A long time ago there was a young man in Liaoyang in the north of China. His father died when he was just a child so he and his mother depended on each other. The young man was very kind to his mother.

Once the mother got ill and the young man was worried about her health. The doctor said she needed to eat fish, but it was winter and all the rivers were frozen. So the young man thought for a long time until at last he found a solution. He went to the river and lay on the ice until it melted from the heat of his body. Then he was able to catch a fish and cure his mother.

How much do you think you know about ice (and ice cream)?

Decide whether the following statements are true or false:

i)   Ice floats in water.
ii)   Ice is white.
iii) Bodies of water freeze from the top down.
iv)   Igloos are made of ice.
v)   About 90% of the mass of an iceberg is beneath the surface of the water.

vi) Icebergs are common in both the Arctic and Antarctic regions.

vii) Both the Arctic and the Antarctic are continents.

viii) Icebergs were responsible for the sinking of the Titanic in 1912.

ix) Ice cream probably originated in Italy in the 17th century.

x) There are eleven players in an ice hockey team.

The answers:

i) True. Because it expands upon freezing.

ii) False. It's colourless and transparent.

iii) True. When the temperature of the surface of an open body of water is reduced toward the freezing point, the surface water becomes denser as it cools, and therefore sinks. It is replaced at the surface by warmer water from beneath. If the water is cooled further, its density decreases and finally ice is formed on the surface.

iv) False. Igloos (Inuit iglu, 'house') are of two kinds: walrus or sealskin tents for summer and huts or houses for winter. Winter houses are usually made of stone, with a driftwood or whalebone frame, chinked and covered with moss or sod. The entrance is a long, narrow passage just high enough to admit a person crawling on hands and knees. During long journeys some Canadian Inuit build winter houses of snow blocks piled in a dome shape. Such snow houses, rare in Greenland and unknown in Alaska, were once permanent winter houses of the Inuit of Central and Eastern Canada.

v) True.

vi) True.

vii) False. Only the Antarctic is one of the seven continents.

viii) True.

ix) False. Ice cream probably originated in China around 2000 BC. It was first made in Italy in the 17th century and appeared in the United States in the early 18th century. The United States ice cream manufacturing industry began in 1851.

x) False. There are only six.

A Guided Visualisation: The Ice Cream Cone

Make yourselves comfortable and close your eyes. Take a few deep breaths to help you relax. Just let your body breathe for you ... and be aware of the air coming in ... and the air going out ... breathing in ... breathing out ... breathing in .... breathing out....

Go inside now. Imagine you're standing in front of a whiteboard with a coloured marker in your hand. Now reach out to the board and draw a large circle on it.... Good.... Now step back and look at the colour and shape of your drawing.

Now imagine an ice cream cone coming to appear inside that circle.... It has all your favourite flavours and toppings.... Perhaps you can see the colours of the ice cream and the cone.... Now reach into the circle and take the ice cream cone into your hand. (Pause.) It's a very warm day and the ice cream is starting to melt ... just a bit ... so you'll want to lick it all around ... tasting the creamy flavour ... and perhaps feeling the coolness on your tongue and the feeling as it slides down your throat.... And it can be fun to take a bite of the ice cream and get a mouthful.... How delicious that can be.... Now it's time to let that image fade.... Just let it disappear,... and as I count slowly from five to one, you can get ready to open your eyes: 5 – 4 – 3 – 2 – 1. Welcome back!

Now take a few minutes in silence to write a description or draw a picture of the ice cream cone you enjoyed. You can then compare your ice creams with the others in the group....

Appendix Two

An Analysis of the Language used in the Scripts

The first point to note about the language of the scripts for visual-isation is the use of the Present Continuous tense. The purpose of this is to imply the process is factual rather than hypothetical and so make it seem more plausible. The process is intended to be something you follow voluntarily, not the result of obligation or the use of force on the part of the guide. This is why the use of the imperative would be inappropriate. The intention is for the 'journey' to be an event in progress and the Present Continuous provides the most effective means of achieving this effect.

Transitional words provide a graceful way of guiding someone into a trance state – going from describing someone's present state to describing the state you want them to go to. Conjunctions such as 'when' or 'as' imply that there is some meaningful relationship between two utterances. "And as I count slowly from one to ten, you go deeper and deeper into a state of total relaxation." There is no relationship between the counting and the state of relaxation. However, it sounds meaningful, and it's the tone of voice and the conjunction 'as' that implies meaning. Linking words like 'while' and 'when' build a relationship between parts of a sentence. The particular relationship is one of time. That relationship allows the listener to move from one idea to another without disjunction. You can take ideas that don't fit together and fit them together this way.

Being 'artfully vague' allows the guide to make statements that sound specific and yet are general enough to be an adequate pace for the listener's experience. Sentences can be constructed in which almost all specific information is deleted. This requires the listener to fill the deletions from his own unique internal experi-ence. There are a number of tools that can be used to achieve this.

Nominalisations are words that take the place of a noun in a sentence, but they are not tangible – they cannot be touched, felt, or heard. They are used as nouns, but they are actually process words. If you say "You have the knowledge you need to …" you've deleted what exactly the subject knows and how he knows it. Nominalisations are effective because they allow the speaker to be vague and require the listener to search through his experience for the most appropriate meaning. They are a means of providing useful instructions without saying something that runs counter to the subject's internal experience.

Unspecified Verbs can also be used to force the listener to supply the meaning in order to understand the sentence. If you say "I want you to learn" you are not specifying how you want the subject to learn, or what specifically you want him to learn about.

Unspecified Referential Index describes the way that the noun being talked about is not specified. A statement like "People can relax" gives the listener the opportunity easily to apply the sentence to themselves in order to understand it.

Deletion refers to sentences in which a major noun phrase is completely missing. In the sentence "I know you are curious" the listener does not know what he is supposedly curious about but can fill in the blanks with whatever is relevant in his experience.

Apart from the use of transition words already mentioned, the strongest kind of linkage makes use of words actually stating causality – causal modelling. "The sound of the music will make you relax more completely" provides an example of this device. The speaker begins with something that is already occurring and connects it to something he wants to occur.

Mind-reading involves acting as if you know the internal experience of the listener and can be an effective tool to build the credibility of the facilitator. "You're probably wondering why you've been called to this place" is an example of how this works.

Lost-performatives are evaluative statements in which the person making the evaluation is missing and can be an effective way of delivering suppositions. An example of this is "it's good that you can relax so easily".

Universal quantifiers that indicate over-generalisations and modal auxiliaries that indicate lack of choice can also be effective tools. "You will never forget these words" and "Notice how you can't open your eyes" provide examples of this.

The way to determine what is presupposed and not open to question in a sentence is to negate the sentence and find out what is still true. The guide can in this way presuppose what he doesn't want to have questioned. "Do you want to sit on a chair or lie down on the floor when you go into a trance?" This directs the listener's attention to the choice of sitting down or not and presupposes that the subject will go into a trance. "Did you know that you spend most of your life in a state of non-ordinary reality?" The only question here is if the listener is aware of the point you are making. The stacking of such presuppositions can make them even more powerful. The following example is taken from *Trance Formations* by Grinder and Bandler:

> "And I don't know how soon you'll realise the learn-
> ings your unconscious has already made, because it's
> not important that you know before you've comfort-
> ably continued the process of relaxation and allowed
> the other you to learn something else of use and
> delight to you."

Indirect elicitation patterns can be used to get specific responses without overtly asking for them. Examples of this include embedded commands and questions such as "You find yourself standing by the shore of a lake" or "I'm curious to know what you would like to gain from the experience". These can be made even more powerful by using analogue marking – setting the directive apart from the rest of the sentence with some non-verbal behaviour, making use of body language, for example. It is interesting to note that when a command is given in its negative form, the positive instruction is generally what is responded to. An example of this could be "I don't want you to feel too relaxed".

Ambiguity is a valuable tool because it results in a mild confusion or disorientation which is useful in inducing altered states. It requires the listener to participate actively in creating the meaning of the message, which increases the likelihood of the meaning being appropriate for him. This can be achieved in many ways including the use of punctuation ambiguity by putting two sentences together that end and begin with the same word. "That's right now you've already begun to relax" is a combination of "That's right," and "Right now you've already begun to relax."

The use of metaphor can also be employed effectively in scripts – attributing qualities to something or someone which by definition could not possess those qualities. By violating selectional restriction, you oblige the listener to find some way of making sense out of what you say. If you say "The moonbeams shower down on you, connecting you with all that is" the listener is likely to make sense out of the statement by equating the "moonbeams" with his own personal power. This is not a conscious process but an automatic way of understanding what is said.

Further scripts designed specifically for classroom use can be found in *A Multiple Intelligences Road To An ELT Classroom* (Crown House Publishing, 1998).

Bibliography

If you are interested in finding out more about the use of guided visualisation and related techniques, including less directed forms of journeying based on shamanic practice, the following books can be recommended:

Abelar, T., (1993) *The Sorcerers' Crossing*, USA: Penguin.

Beaver, D., (1994) *Lazy Learning*, UK: Element Books.

Berman, M., (1998) *A Multiple Intelligences Road To An ELT Classroom*, UK: Crown House Publishing.

Bleakley, A., (1984) *Fruits of the Moon Tree*, UK: Gateway Books.

Castaneda, C., (1970) *The Teachings of Don Juan*, UK: Penguin.

Castaneda, C., (1991) *A Separate Reality*, USA: Pocket Books.

Castaneda, C., (1993) *Journey to Ixtlan*, USA: Washington Square Press.

Castaneda, C., (1976) *Tales of Power*, UK: Penguin.

Castaneda, C., (1979) *The Second Ring of Power*, UK: Penguin.

Castaneda, C., (1982) *The Eagle's Gift*, UK: Penguin.

Castaneda, C., (1984) *The Fire From Within*, UK: Black Swan.

Castaneda, C., (1988) *The Power of Silence*, UK: Black Swan.

Castaneda, C., (1993)*The Art of Dreaming*, UK: HarperCollins.

Diamond, J., (1997) *Life Energy and The Emotions*, UK: Eden Grove Editions.

Dennison, P., (1981) *Switching On*, USA: Edu-Kinesthetics, Inc.

Edwards, G., (1991) *Living Magically*, UK: Piatkus.

Edwards, G., (1993) *Stepping Into the Magic*, UK: Piatkus.

Eliade, M., (1989) *Shamanism*, USA: Penguin.

Field, L., (1993) *Creating Self Esteem*, UK: Element.

Fletcher, M., (1995) *The Suggestopedic Elephant*, UK: English Experience.

Freeman Dhority, L. & Jensen, E., (1998) *Joyful Fluency*, USA: The Brain Store, Inc.

Gagan, J., (1998) *Journeying – Where Shamanism and Psychology Meet*, USA: Rio Chama Publications.

Gallwey, W. T., (1975) *The Inner Game of Tennis*, UK: Pan Books.

Gallwey, W. T., (1977) *The Inner Game of Skiing*, UK: Pan Books.

Gallwey, W. T., (1981) *The Inner Game of Golf*, UK: Pan Books.

Galyean, B., (1983) *Mind Sight*, USA: Center for Integrative Learning.

Gardner, H., (1993) *Multiple Intelligences,* USA: Basic Books.

Grinder, J. & Bandler, R., (1979) *Frogs into Princes,* USA: Real People Press.

Grinder, J. & Bandler, R., (1981) *Trance Formations,* USA: Real People Press.

Hager, M., (1994) *Target Fluency,* (1994) USA: Metamorphous Press.

Halifax, J., (1982) *Shaman – The Wounded Healer,* UK: Thames & Hudson.

Harman, W. & Rheingold, H., (1985) *Higher Creativity,* USA: J.P. Tarcher.

Harner, M., (1990) *The Way of the Shaman,* USA: Harper & Row.

Hay, L., (1988) *You Can Heal Your Life,* UK: Eden Grove Editions.

Holdway, A., (1995) *Kinesiology,* UK: Element Books.

Houston, J., (1987) *The Search for the Beloved,* USA: J.P. Tarcher.

Hull, J., (1997) *On Sight and Insight: A Journey Into The World of Blindness,* UK: Oneworld Publications.

Ingerman, S., (1998) *Soul Retrieval,* USA: Harper.

Ingerman, S., (1993) *Welcome Home,* USA: Harper.

Jensen, E., (1995) *Brain Based Teaching and Learning,* USA: The Brain Store, Inc.

Jensen, E., (1998) *Trainer's Bonanza,* USA: The Brain Store, Inc.

Jung, C., (1964) *Man and his Symbols,* USA: Doubleday.

Lacroix, N. & Gallagher-Mundy, C., (1995) *Relaxation,* UK: Thorsons.

Mindell, A., (1993) *The Shaman's Body,* USA: Harper.

Murdoch, M., (1987) *Spinning Inward,* USA: Shambhala Publications.

Noah, G., (1995) *The Magical Classroom,* USA: Zephyr Press.

Parfitt, W., (1990) *The Elements of Psychosynthesis,* UK: Element Books.

Parkin, M., (1998) *Tales for Trainers,* UK: Kogan Page.

Revell, J. & Norman, S., (1997) *In Your Hands,* UK: Saffire Press.

Revell, J. & Norman, S., (1999) *Handing Over,* UK: Saffire Press.

Shannon Campbell, M., (1997) *The Well Formed Story,* USA: Meta*Force.

Singer & Switzer (1980) *Mind-Play: The Creative Uses of Fantasy,* UK: Prentice-Hall.

Smith, A., (1996) *Accelerated Learning in the Classroom,* UK: Network Educational Press.

Smith, A., (1998) *Accelerated Learning in Practice,* UK: Network Educational Press.

Walsh, R., (1990) *The Spirit of Shamanism,* UK: Aquarian Press.

Zdenek, M., (1995) *The Right Brain Experience,* USA: Two Roads Press.

Other titles from

Crown House Publishing
www.crownhouse.co.uk

The Magic of Metaphor
77 Stories for Teachers, Trainers and Thinkers
Nick Owen

The Magic of Metaphor presents a collection of stories designed to engage, inspire and transform the listener and the reader. Some of the stories motivate, some are spiritual, and some provide strategies for excellence. All promote positive feelings, encouraging confidence, direction and vision.

Containing sixteen suggestions (or tips) for effective storytelling, advice on organisation, style and storytelling skills, and a selection of stories that can be adapted and developed, *The Magic of Metaphor* is an inspirational sourcebook for counsellors, health workers, psychologists, professional speakers, managers, leaders and NLP practitioners, as well as for teachers, trainers, therapists. Providing tools that assist people in making beneficial changes in their lives, the stories contained in this book will bring pleasure and power to all those that listen to or read them.

PAPERBACK   320 PAGES   ISBN: 1899836705

A Multiple Intelligences Road To An ELT Classroom
Michael Berman

Written and designed for TEFL teachers, this is a visually appealing, thoroughly practical resource full of exercises, activities, stories, visualisations, puzzles and information for immediate use in the classroom. Organised into ten clearly defined units, it deals in turn with each of the eight intelligences – logical/mathematical, verbal/linguistic, visual/spatial, bodily/kinesthetic, musical/rhythmic, interpersonal, intrapersonal and naturalist – providing exercises and advice for teaching using each of them. Built on sound grammatical foundations, the book contains all a teacher will need to keep students challenged and learning in the style that suits them best. Covering all essential areas of ELT, *A Multiple Intelligences Road To An ELT Classroom* makes teaching easily accessible, compelling and FUN! An extremely versatile book, this can also be used as an activities resource for teachers of English as a first language.

PAPERBACK   216 PAGES   ISBN: 1899836233

Orders to:

The Anglo American Book Company Ltd.

Crown Buildings, Bancyfelin, Carmarthen, Wales, SA33 5ND, UK

Tel: +44(0)1267 211880/211886 Fax: +44(0)1267 211882
(Lines open 9am – 5.30pm Mon – Fri)

E-mail address: books@anglo-american.co.uk

www.anglo-american.co.uk

Or visit the
Crown House Publishing website at:

www.crownhouse.co.uk